Praise for
The Song of Father-Son: Men in Search of The Blessing

The time has never been more right for telling the story of the Unblessed son. With compassion and humor, Peter reveals his own, often painful, story of growing up. Through his personal courage and determination, he reveals how he has transformed himself. Possibly more important is how Peter is raising his own young son, Henry. It is here that he offers his hard won wisdom to fathers everywhere: the legacy of a Blessed son.

—**Rich Tosi,** co-founder of the New Warrior Training Adventure and the Mankind Project

The Song of Father-Son *should be read by every son who has ever ached for his father's unconditional love and approval, and by every father who has ever found himself somehow unable to convey the depth of his love to his son. With insight, wit and heartfelt prose, Peter Putnam has given us a book that is itself a blessing, a testament to the power that we as men have to heal each other, and ourselves.*

—**Phil Taylor,** Senior Writer, *Sports Illustrated*

It's a moving tribute to his father, a moving story about his experience…and it drew me in—not in small part because so much of it is my story, too! And the love of what he's doing in writing it all down makes the narrative glow.

—**Peter Clothier,** author of *While I Am Not Afraid: Secrets of a Man's Heart*

This is a MUST read for every woman, particularly mothers of sons. Learning about and accepting the importance of the father's blessing is a gift each woman can give her sons, her husband, brothers, or any man she knows.

—**Char Tosi,** RN, MS, author of *Woman Within Training, Mother's Shadow Workshop* and co-author of *Your Mother's Pillow* and *The Couples Weekend*

The Song of Father-Son *is a unique blend of autobiography, poetry, and personal narrative, which creates one man's attempt to gain some emotional literacy and personal healing around his relationship with his father, especially now that he has a son of his own.*

—**Dr. Edward Read Barton** (Ed.) of *Mythopoetic Perspectives of Men's Healing Work: An Anthology for Therapists and Others*

The Song of Father-Son

The Song of Father-Son

◆

Men in Search of The Blessing

Peter H. Putnam

iUniverse, Inc.
New York Lincoln Shanghai

The Song of Father-Son
Men in Search of The Blessing

Copyright © 2006 by Peter H. Putnam

All rights reserved. No part of this book may be used or reproduced by any means, graphic, electronic, or mechanical, including photocopying, recording, taping or by any information storage retrieval system without the written permission of the publisher except in the case of brief quotations embodied in critical articles and reviews.

iUniverse books may be ordered through booksellers or by contacting:

iUniverse
2021 Pine Lake Road, Suite 100
Lincoln, NE 68512
www.iuniverse.com
1-800-Authors (1-800-288-4677)

Front cover illustration by Mario Moore
Front and back cover photo by Vince Mariano

ISBN-13: 978-0-595-37733-6 (pbk)
ISBN-13: 978-0-595-67555-5 (cloth)
ISBN-13: 978-0-595-82112-9 (ebk)
ISBN-10: 0-595-37733-5 (pbk)
ISBN-10: 0-595-67555-7 (cloth)
ISBN-10: 0-595-82112-X (ebk)

Printed in the United States of America

*Dedicated to my father, Peter Henry Putnam Sr. (1934–1998),
and to my son, Henry Michael James Putnam (born June 8, 2005).*

May this book Bless you both.

Contents

Foreword... xix
Introduction xxi

UNBLESSED SONS

Dead Boy Walking... 3
The Father-Hole... 6
A Man Alone... 7
"Father And Son".. 9
Absent Homer, Lost Bart...................................... 11
The City of Lost Sons (poem)................................. 13
The World of Unblessed Sons.................................. 15

WHAT THE BLESSING ISN'T...AND IS

The Lamp... 19
The Curse.. 20
The Metamorphosis.. 22
The Fight.. 23
Pass This Test... 25
"You're Gay!".. 26
Now That's a Man!.. 27

Stoney & Wojo 28
Our Father Who Art in Heaven 29
Sometimes I Feel like a Fatherless Child 30
David 32
Unconditional Love 33
Enough, Now 34
Christmas Lights 35
Marathon Man 36
Man Enough 39
My Blessing 41
Being Heard 42
In a Nutshell 44

BLESSING OUR EMOTIONS

A Man's Best Friend 47
Mad, Sad, Glad, Fear, Shame 49
Pitch-and-Catch 51
American Men's Lives 53
Recipe to Make a Man Cry 54
Johnny Carson 55
A Man's Anger 57
Men's Rage 59
Surprised by Joy 62
The "Be A Man" Box 64
"I am not worthy!" 66

"It's not your fault" 68

BLESSING OUR BODY

My Father Had a 4-Foot Penis (poem) 73

Men's Bodies 76

No Pain, No Gain 77

Back Pain 79

Boy in a Rowboat 81

Is There Life After Basketball? 82

Hugs 84

The Catcher in the Rye 85

Sexual Abuse 87

Penis Size 89

Boxing Gloves 91

BLESSING THE GOOD BOY, THE BAD BOY, AND EVERY BOY IN BETWEEN

Dylan 95

The Good Boy 96

The Bad Boy 97

The Eternal Boy 98

Mama's Boy 100

The Man of the House 102

Salvation Son 103

Pete Nice 104

Poor Me! 106

My Little Boy 107

BLESSING THE INITIATION OF MEN

Driving 111
When I Became a Man (at 42). .112
Coaches. 114
My Vietnam 116
Birth & War 118
Kill Your Mother, Marry Your Father 120
Umbilical Cord 122

BLESSING OUR HEROES

Arnie's Army. 125
What do Tiger and Michael and Lance Have in Common?. 127
Pistol Pete 129
Jesus, Brother. 131
The Woods Beyond my Father's House. 132
Malcolm X. 134
Iron Robert 136

BLESSING OUR FAMILY

The Letter. 141
"Son". 142
"Bro". 143
"Dude!". 144
Uncles 145

Cousins..146
Dean...147
Gramps..148

BLESSING OUR SHADOW

Burying Houdini (poem)......................153
Men and Our Shadow..........................156
My Mid-life Crisis...............................160
Black Men.......................................162
Cops & Doctors.................................164
Big Guys, Big Stories...........................165
Stan the Man Talks Back 167
Bullies...172
George Bush & Me.............................174
Forgive Me, I Knew Not What I Was Doing 175
The Father of All Projects......................176
Truth Junkie....................................178
The Rescuer Par Excellance....................180
Swing Low, Sweet Chariot 182
Loving What Is.................................184

BLESSING OUR WOMEN

Elmer Ave.......................................189
Disappearing Men..............................191
Woman-Hunger................................193

Wise Women...195
What About My Mother?.....................................196

BLESSING A CIRCLE OF MEN

Howard, Sam, & Fran......................................201
AA..202
Guy Banter..204
"Gentleman, welcome to Fight Club".........................206
The King's Round..209
A Circle of Men...210
Me and Seventy Men Had Ourselves a Weekend (poem).........212

BLESSING OUR FATHERS

The Love Song of Father-Son..............................217
Who's Your Daddy?...220
Go Gentle into That Good Night............................221
Blessings My Father Did Give Me...........................223
Sweet Forgiveness...225
It's Not Your Fault: Take 2...............................226
"Sometimes You Can't Make It On Your Own".................227
My Father's Eulogy..229

BLESSING FATHERHOOD

Six Years Soon (poem)....................................233
What Will I Be When I Grow Up?............................234
Legacy..236

Martha's Vineyard.................................. 238
Present Dads....................................... 240

BLESSING OUR WORLD, BLESSING OUR FUTURE

My Father's Grave 243
Now What?... 245
A Man's Mission................................... 248
The Power of a Son's Imagination.................. 250
Your Father's Blessing............................ 253
New Warriors...................................... 255
The Blessing (poem)............................... 258
The New Founding Fathers 260
Epilogue: "Blessing Henry" (poem)................. 261

Appendix   Writing Your Way Toward The Blessing 263
Select Bibliography............................... 269

Acknowledgements

Brendan, Jimmy, Sam: In a world where men are often alone, you have been in my life for three decades, spinning theories, trading stories, shooting baskets, and most of all, modeling what it means to be honorable men. I respect you, I love you, I thank you.

My New Warrior brothers Joseph, John, Dave, Todd, Steve, Ken, Gary: Thanks to your audacious authenticity, I leave Joseph's basement most Monday nights a stronger, more loving man. And to my New Warrior Elders—Rich, Steve, Tim, Dan, Russ, Ralph, Ed, Tom, Peter—who have blessed me with their kingly wisdom.

Paul: We dug forts together and buried a father. Brothers from the beginning, brothers for life.

Mom: In my senior year English class you encouraged me to take a stab at poetry—and I've been writing poems ever since. And it was also from you that I learned the importance of going inside, where spirit lives.

Nancy, Judith, Chris: Every man needs a good therapist. I've had three.

Julia: Wife, best friend, lover of my sun and my shadow—not to mention editor extraordinaire—you are the powerful, loving woman I have the privilege of loving. Thank you for hanging in there long enough for me to become the man you knew I could become, and the father—oh, this beautiful Henry adventure together!—I am becoming.

Foreword

During my 20 years experience as a facilitator at ManKind Project workshops, I have witnessed how deeply and painfully men's souls have been wounded by fathers who loved their sons but simply did not know how to bless them. These sons are now the men who are business leaders, factory workers, lawyers, doctors, and tradesmen. They are sons who are now husbands and fathers. They are the men you meet everyday.

In the last 3 decades our culture has become increasingly aware of the toll that unblessed sons have on society. Men who were not blessed by their fathers become dangerous men. They want to prove that they are worthy of the blessings they never received. Their search for the blessing may take the form of a quest for money or conquering woman or even totally dropping out of society. It is a fruitless search because the blessing is not "out there". Many authors, including Robert Bly and Robert Moore, have noted that the bond between father and son is critical for the son as well as the whole of society. Every son yearns for a deep and loving connection with his father. Indeed, the emotional and spiritual health of any son is critically dependent on the bond with his father. A healthy son grows to be a mature and responsible man.

The world is truly in great need of mature men who were blessed and respected by their fathers. Unfortunately, modern culture places little value on this aspect of the father-son relationship.

Some men are changing their relationships with their sons. One of those men is Peter Putnam. He has confronted the issue directly with his book, *THE SONG OF FATHER-SON: Men in Search of The Blessing*. The time has never been more right for telling the story of the Unblessed son. With compassion and humor, Peter reveals his own, often painful, story of growing up. Through his personal courage and determination, he reveals how he has transformed himself. Possibly more important is how Peter is raising his own young son, Henry. It is here that he offers his hard won wisdom to fathers everywhere: the legacy of a Blessed son.

Rich Tosi
Co-founder of the Mankind Project and the New Warrior Training Adventure

Introduction

I see scared boys everywhere.

I see them walking down Detroit streets in low-slung jeans and blank faces. I see them in the front rows and back rows of my community college classroom. I see them at the head of churches; I see them at the head of unions and at the head of banks. I see them in Hollywood; I see them in the NBA; I see them in the White House. I am a scared boy—my father dead, a baby coming. Scared boys, all of us, searching for, dying for, all the while pretending not to care about, the one thing we most wanted and never got…

The Blessing. We crave The Blessing of our father. Our father, whoever he is, wherever he's been, hugging us close and saying these simple, magical words:

Son, I'm proud of you. You have all you need to be a strong, loving man.

My whole life—this whole book—is about that hug, those words.

I believe if a man finds a way to hear those words, he will be healed. If he fails to find a way to hear those words—and ultimately, to say them to himself and to other scared boys—he will continue to suffer as a man.

Does that feel true? Right now, as you read these words, does that feel true to you? Imagine your father, dead or alive, imagine him right now, pulling you into his chest, into his distinctive smell and bulk and warmth, pulling you close, and in a clear, sincere voice, telling you:

Son, my son, you have all you need to be a strong, loving man. You can stop trying so hard. You can stop now. Enough. You ARE that man you are trying so hard to be. You are enough. Do you hear me?

Listen to him. Let it sink in. How crazy it is, that we resist the very medicine we most need to heal. We don't believe it; our whole messed-up lives, our insides, tell us it can't be true.

But listen to him. Listen. He's saying it again.

Son, really: You have all you need to be a strong and loving man. You've had it from the beginning, from birth, from before birth. You came out of the womb and into my arms with that in you: your strength, your love, your manhood. No woman has to bestow that on you. No job. No home run. No bank account. No drug. Believe it, please believe it. From the beginning, from the very beginning. Forgive me for not telling you. Forgive me for not gathering other men, my friends, elders, a tribe of men and telling you when you were twelve and ready to enter manhood. Forgive me for not telling you every day of your life. Just because I failed to tell you doesn't mean it's not true. My father failed to tell me, and his father probably failed to tell him. Somehow, somewhere, this horrible cycle of Unblessed sons got started. But this is the truth—you have all you need to be a strong, loving man—and I am telling you this so you can tell your son.

Maybe it's impossible for you to even imagine that your father could ever say these words. Maybe if he did, he would be, by such an act, someone else—a loving, healing father where your father was a curser, a hurter, a drinker, a deserter, a hitter, a fucker, a whiner, a loser, a terror. Or maybe you sensed your father truly wanted to say this to you, that somewhere in him The Blessing for you existed, but he didn't have the courage, didn't have the strength, didn't have the skills, didn't have the self-love to say it.

That's the dilemma most men find themselves in today: for whatever reason, our fathers were unable to give us The Blessing. We are the Unblessed sons of Unblessed sons. And because we failed to get The Blessing, we feel more like boys than men, angry or depressed or sad or ashamed, with a huge father-hole in our life which we continue to try to fill up with booze, with sex, with food, with books, with God, with work…

So what is an Unblessed boy to do?

This book is all about what we can do. This book is about discovering and recovering The Blessing that is our birthright as men. This book is about finding our father, creating the fathering we need to confirm on us the truth of who we are: that we are strong; that we are loving and worthy of love. That we are men. And this book is also about passing The Blessing on: telling our sons, telling other boys, telling other men that they, too, have all they need to be strong, loving men. In this way, we break the cycle of Unblessed sons—and what I suspect are connected cycles of alcoholism, abuse, racism, misogyny, homophobia, and depression—that goes back in most families for generations.

On one level, this book is the story of my relationship with my father. I wrote much of it in the first two trimesters of my wife's pregnancy, perhaps trying to secure The Blessing before I become a father myself. But in reality, I have been writing it all my life, even before I chose my father as my "biography" subject in eighth-grade English. More than any other person, any other thing, any event, my father has defined my life. I am who I am largely because of who he was, and who he wasn't; I am the boy who grew out of his strengths and his weaknesses. His illness and death seven years ago, when I was 38, was my wake-up call to explore our life together.

The Blessing is the most significant thing to come out of that exploration. That, and a deepening, hard-earned forgiveness for an Unblessed father who was unable to give The Blessing to his son.

My hope is that what you find here may be the story, or part of the story, of your relationship with your father. Some of these pieces may speak to you, some may not. Some may have the sting or sweetness of truth…some may not. What I've tried to do here is gather pieces of our fathers—pieces of the fathers too wounded to Bless, and pieces of the fathers healed enough to Bless. I have come to believe both parts, wounded wounder and healing healer, are in each father—buried beneath a blizzard of pain and shame, perhaps, but present nonetheless.

And as a man recognizes the wounded wounder and the healing healer that is his father, as he opens to hear The Blessing from his father, from other men, from himself, he begins to move through the world like a Blessed son. Such a Blessed son will not feel the need to measure himself incessantly against other men. Much of the toxic shame that poisoned his relationships, and poisoned his own body and soul, will have dissipated. A Blessed son will be able to recognize his shame, his anger, his sadness, his fear, his joy—and welcome them all. His body, long a source of shame—of not enoughness, of too muchness—will begin to feel like the wise, durable companion it was meant to be. A Blessed son is man enough.

For The Blessing isn't about changing who we are.

The Blessing isn't something added to us, something implanted in us; some new part to replace an old part.

The Blessing is about recognizing who we already are: the man-seed in us that only needs a father's watering. We thought we were all winter, all cold and housebound. And then suddenly, the second we hear our father, or an elder, or a man tell us we have all we need to be powerful, loving men…we feel the spring open up inside us. The blooming.

The Song of Father-Son consists of 130 pieces organized in fourteen chapters. Although many of these pieces allude to my father, the first piece of each chapter is explicitly a memoir entry. In rough chronological order, these italicized writings trace the arc of my life with my father, from the late 1960s-mid 1970s growing up in Schenectady, NY—"Dead Boy Walking," "Dylan," "Driving"; through college ("The Letter"); his intense illness ("The Love Song of Father-Son"); his death in Salem, South Carolina in 1998 ("Go Gentle Into That Good Night"); and my/our rebirth over the last seven years ("Six Years Soon," "My Father's Grave"). Looking at them now, I am awed by how much I don't know, and therefore, couldn't write about the life of this immensely complex man. That is one of the paradoxes of the Unblessed son: we always want to know more about the lives of our fathers, but, by virtue of being Unblessed themselves, our fathers often didn't have the means to tell us, and sometimes didn't know themselves.

Chapter one, "Unblessed Sons," depicts the hellish, hole-ish world most scared boys inhabit. If you're addicted—to booze, to food, to cigarettes, to work, to sex, to sports, to God—you're probably an Unblessed son: we fill our father-hole with whatever we can. And though we may frequently be around men, we are most often men alone. This is nothing to be ashamed of, though many of us are filled with shame; this is simply where we begin our journey back to our fathers and back to the The Blessing.

Growing up, did you feel as much or more cursed by your father as blessed? In this second chapter, "What The Blessing Isn't…And Is," I introduce The Blessing's opposite, The Curse, and its diverse manifestations, including moments from my childhood ("The Lamp") and my classroom ("The Metamorphosis"). I then follow with more and more concrete representations of The Blessing itself—from "Now *That's* A Man!" to "Marathon Man." The Blessing reverses The Curse: it gives us back our Bigness.

Are your emotions generally limited to angry and numb? Is your body not enough—or too much? Chapters three and four form the core of The Blessing. Since most of us are afraid of our emotions and ashamed of our bodies, "Blessing Our Emotions" and "Blessing Our Bodies" are the two fundamental areas a father must bless in order for a son to feel whole.

Chapter five, "Blessing The Good Boy, The Bad Boy, And Every Boy In Between," examines some typical roles Unblessed sons end up playing. For me, it was Pete Nice—maybe for you, it was the Bad Boy or the Eternal Boy or Mama's Boy. In all these cases, each of us attempted to earn what The Blessing would have given us for free: the unconditional love of our father. And as I discuss in this chapter's final piece, that love, more than anything, was our Little Boy's deepest need.

When did your Little Boy stop running your life: when did you become a man? Can you put a finger on a precise moment or ritual when you stepped into your manhood? Or maybe, as is true for many men, that moment hasn't yet arrived for you and you still feel, and often act, like a boy? Chapter 6, featuring "When I Became a Man (at 42)" and "Kill Your Mother, Marry Your Father," emphasizes the absolute need for "boys," at whatever age, to be initiated into manhood by strong, loving men. Here, I also explore several initiatory dead-ends—"Coaches" and war.

How The Blessing plays itself out in those close to us and those far away is the subject of the next two chapters, "Blessing Our Heroes" and "Blessing Our Family." Here, I examine the gold and shadow—the hidden "positive" and "negative" energies inside us—we project outward on sons, brothers, uncles, cousins, grandfathers, and guys—as well as the gold and shadow I have heaped onto my own assortment of "heroes" like Pistol Pete Maravich, Tiger Woods, Michael Jordan, Lance Armstrong, Jesus, Malcolm X, and Robert Bly.

I continue that examination in "Blessing Our Shadow," as I dip into the places in my own life—from "My Mid-Life Crisis" to "Black Men" and "George Bush and Me"—where flickerings of Blessing and Unblessing live. As boys, we stuffed what we had to, the good and the bad, in order to get whatever we could of our father's love; as men, particularly as middle-aged men, we can make the journey within to recover our gold and restore our wholeness.

If you have long been searching for The Right Woman to "complete" you, the next chapter is for you. In "Blessing Our Women," I debunk the idea that a woman can give a man The Blessing, while honoring the other blessings women *can* bestow upon men. The same, I would add, goes for mothers, which is the topic of the chapter's final piece, "What About My Mother?"

Somewhere, at some time in your life, you probably experienced the connective power of men coming together for a purpose. Maybe it was in a football stadium, a church, an AA meeting, or on a picket line, a sports team, or a work project; most likely, it rocked you deeply, and ended too quickly. Chapter eleven, "Blessing A Circle of Men," illustrates the primal power of men coming together—not only for purposes of initiation into manhood, but also for continuing growth and blessing as men, with men, by men.

If you have a father, are a father, are afraid to be a father, or maybe all three, the next two chapters should provide plenty of thought fodder: chapter twelve is dedicated to my father, from "Blessings My Father Did Give Me," to his final blessing, "My Father's Eulogy"; chapter thirteen, to my own impending fatherhood and on my great hope in "Present Fathers." These pieces suggest that beyond the pain song, the sad song, the angry song…the song of father-son is, finally, primordially, blessedly, a love song.

The last chapter of *The Song of Father-Son* offers the most practical suggestions for getting The Blessing ("Now What?" and "Your Father's Blessing"), an introduction to a model of manhood that I believe is beginning to replace the John Wayne Old Warrior model ("New Warriors"), and a vision of what a world of Blessing sons could create ("The New Founding Fathers"). The Appendix, "Writing Your Way Toward The Blessing," offers some concrete prompts to resurrect memories of your father, and, through letters, to hear the words you were dying to hear from him and were longing to say to him. In addition, the Appendix has some questions tied to each of the book's chapters; feel free to dip into them at any time and try your hand. Finally, a Select Bibliography offers the books that most inspired my own quest to find the deepest truths about fathers and sons and masculinity.

Throughout this book, there are numerous references to the Mankind Project and its New Warrior Training Adventure (NWTA) weekend. Begun in 1985 by three men—Ron Hering, Bill Kauth, and the man who was generous enough to write the "Foreword" to this book, Rich Tosi—the NWTA weekend is offered throughout the United States, as well as in nine other countries; over 30,000 men have completed it. Through a synchronized weaving of games, group discussions, guided imagery visualizations, journaling, and individual work, the New Warrior Training invites men to make the journey from head to heart, and to celebrate their passage into manhood. The NWTA, then, is a traditional masculine initiation, but geared to the modern-day man. For more information on the Mankind Project and the New Warrior Training Adventure weekend, I invite you to visit our website: www.mkp.org.

But no words can adequately summarize what my own weekend in June, 2001 and my subsequent work in the Mankind Project has meant in terms of my understanding of accountability and integrity, connection to feelings, leadership, fatherhood, and the blessing of Elders—in short, of what it means to be a man in this world. In the last four years, I have staffed a weekend, attended a dozen Mankind Project-generated workshops, circled up and heard the inner truths of hundreds of men, and perhaps most importantly, been present at close to two hundred meetings with my "I-group"—with five men I did my weekend with in 2001, and three other initiated men who have since joined us. It is here, each Monday night, 7:00–9:30pm, in Joseph's Ferndale, Michigan basement, that the eight of us have talked and been heard; have cried and been hugged; have yelled and been honored. It is here, "on the carpet," where I have worked through much of the anguish of being an Unblessed son—and where I have facilitated some of the same healing in other men. It is here where I have both received The Blessing and given The Blessing.

You can read *The Song of Father-Son* straight through…or you could randomly open it before bed, sip a quick cup of strong, masculine truth—and close it for the night. At the end of most of the pieces is an italicized Blessing. You might consider reading this part out loud, letting the words move through your body, as you imagine your father saying them to you, or you to your father, or to your son, or to a man or boy in your life.

Once we were scared boys. Now we are Kings: powerful and loving, generous and generative. For we are Blessed, and we can Bless. And in so Blessing, we break the cycle and we change the world…one Unblessed son at a time.

UNBLESSED SONS

Dead Boy Walking

My father is taking me into our Cortland Dr. backyard in the summer of 1967, me in front holding a Mickey Mouse cape, him behind, a chair and dog clippers in his hand.

I am a dead boy walking.

He sets the green kitchen chair down facing the house; he presses me into it with one of his great, brown hands; he swings the Mickey Mouse cape over me with an executioner's ease, fastens it so tight against my throat I can feel my Adam's apple's every bob. My nose and eyes are already itchy, I'm ready to cry. It's impossible to cry.

I think of my brother waiting to be next, off around the side of the house, digging angrily in the dirt.

The late morning sun burns sweat down my face.

Then my gut jumps when, behind me, he clicks on the dog clippers—those horrible vibrating metal teeth. Again, from above, I feel the pressure of his enormous hand on the soft top of my head—golf calluses rough on my scalp—pressing down, pressing down, pressing down on my weak eight-year-old neck. Realizing he could snap it—like that!—if he wanted to. If I gave him a reason to.

I try to keep my eyes open, to be brave, but the awful clipper buzz—closer and closer—twitches them closed. I see the red-orange burn of the sun on the back of my eyelids. My legs are clenched tight like terrible times on the toilet, my toes fetaled inside my Keds.

I cringe at contact: metal teeth touching down, sizzling, biting, my hair putting up tiny resistance. Then the first strip cut like a snow blower's path down a driveway. Like an ax through white wood. Like a bulldozer's iron jaws through small pine. I imagine the pale glint of my skull as the black hair, a spring's worth, slides off, catches in the sweat of my face, in the curve of my nose, in the soft of my throat. When he scrapes and scrapes the electric metal teeth across the softness of my scalp, I want to cry, to cry out, to scream for him to Stop, just stop, please stop!

But my words, and my tears, get swallowed up some place deep.

Then, for a moment, relief. My father is directly in front of me now, blocking the unbearable sun. I love him now, when he's blocking the sun, when my father's great white t-shirted body shields me from the burning sun. But then he moves behind me again, the sun sears my face, the sweat starts again, the chopped hair unbearably itchy on my nose, my cheeks, my neck. But I'm armless, my hands pinned under the cape. It would take a courage and strength I don't have to work them free and scratch.

Through eyes flushed with sun and shame, I see quills of hair—black needles—clots of hair—black wounds—curls of hair—black clouds—all over Mickey.

I love my hair. Like Samson who I had heard about in church, my hair makes me feel strong. After this, tomorrow, when I look into the mirror: I am a clown, a pathetic clown, ears suddenly enlarged, nose Pinocchioing when it shouldn't have. I don't tell lies! I only tell the truth! Why is this happening? What did I do wrong? Why is my father doing this to me?

I see my mother watching from the kitchen window. Washing dishes, watching me. I see guilt in her eyes, I'm sure of it, though I can't really see her eyes. She didn't do anything to stop this—what could she do? And maybe, secretly, she even likes it. Yes, keep it short, he'll always be mine if you keep it short, keep him ugly.

The neighbors, are the neighbors watching? I don't care, I can't even bear to think that they might be. They'll see the results soon enough, the whole world will see what happened to me in this backyard.

All around me, my hair is falling. With each buzzed clump, I am falling, my soul mowed down. I am a dirty lawn, a sheared lamb, Abraham's son. I am the answer to all the hippies who fly their freak flags at the world. I am this forever weak son beneath his father's angry shears. Scalped.

At the end, your rough fingers undo the cape. You swat stray hairs off the back of my neck with the back of your hand. There is not an ounce of comfort in your face or words. You only say the most horrible thing you can say: "Send your brother back here." Me, why me? I want to run and bury my head somewhere deep. I don't want to have any part of this. "Send your brother back here." I don't want to get my brother, I don't want to help you do your dirty work! Do it your own god damn self!

But I am the polite, perfectly behaved boy in a world gone mad. My father still knows best, and I do exactly as he tells me. I walk to the side of the house, head up but eyes down, tears leaking out now that he can't see me.

I find my brother looking down, moving things around in the dirt. "Your turn," I manage to say. There is no glee in it, no ha ha! He doesn't look at me; he doesn't try to tell me that it looks OK. He picks up a clump of dirt and throws it down. Then he heads for the backyard and I head up to my room.

I am no longer a dead boy walking. For the next thirty-five years, I will be a dead boy running...running away from the pain, away from my father...all the while running just as frantically, just as fast toward him...a son, a lost running son who will bump into other lost running sons, all of us hating our fathers, loving our fathers...all *of us searching for strong, loving men who will tell us we are strong, loving men...all of us searching for The Blessing.*

The Father-Hole

Unblessed sons are holes. Big, gaping holes. Walking abysses. Ghosts. Outside, we're all steel; inside, we're bottomless fatherless pits.

And we're searching ravenously for anything to fill up our father-hole.

Booze.

Sex.

Food.

Books.

God.

Work.

You name it. Anything to feel full, solid, strong.

And loved. Because right now, as we are, we believe we are finally and totally unlovable—empty, insubstantial, weak.

Robert Bly calls it father-hunger. We are hungry for our fathers, hungry for contact with them, conversation—and ultimately, Blessing. If that Blessing doesn't happen when we're boys, if no man tells us we have all it takes to be strong, loving men, we logically, psychologically, tragically assume we are, and always will be, weak and unlovable boys—holes who will fill up on anything, absolutely anything, in order to feel like men.

The Blessing doesn't "add" anything. It's not a matter of injecting masculinity into an empty body. It merely recognizes the solidity that is already there in a boy or a man. Or at the most, it's like a ray of sun or a drop of water on a seed—a stimulant to built-in growth.

Son, I know you feel as empty as an empty football stadium. I know that you think you will always be weak, always be a boy, forever unlovable. I know that you have already tried to fill up on anything you could get your hands on, anything that would make you feel stronger, more of a man. And that none of that finally worked. Trust me when I tell you you already have all you need—all the power, all the love. It doesn't have to be poured into you—it's already inside you. You are not a hole, you are a house full of gold. Before, now, and forever, you are a house full of gold.

A Man Alone

I lived across the street from Ron for ten years. He was a good man. He helped the neighborhood kids when their bikes broke down. He fixed my lawn mower, strung up my kitchen light, fed my cat when I went out of town.

And he drank.

Started early, kept at it, drunk and numb by sunset. Ron wasn't one of those angry drunks—more a friendly drunk, who then became a sad drunk, who finally ended up an ashamed drunk.

There was a world of hurt wrapped up tight inside him. We had known each other six or seven years before he told me about his older brother dying in a motorcycle accident when Ron was in his teens. It was obvious he looked up to this brother, and in some way I never understood, even felt responsible somehow for his death. When he told me that day in my backyard, he was on the edge of tears.

"I bet you didn't cry at his funeral," I said softly.

Ron shook his head.

"I bet you've never cried about it."

Ron shook his head again. And he couldn't cry that day either, I'm sad to say.

He had a strong, supportive woman in his life, but that's not where we get The Blessing. What he also needed were men in his life—men who could show him it was safe to cry, men who could bless him.

Like so many men, Ron was a man alone.

I invited him to a "Head, Heart, & Soul" I was doing, a get-together to interest men to sign up for the New Warrior Training Adventure weekend. It was scheduled for a Sunday afternoon; on Sunday morning, I saw the ambulance pull up in front of his house. When they stretchered him out, he looked more dead than alive. There were several pools of blood and bile on his living room floor.

Six months later, I saw him for the last time. He was lying in the V.A. hospital, unrecognizably old, unspeakably skeletal. With tears in my eyes, I told him he was a good friend, a good man.

He shook his head. "I was bad!" he said with surprising volume.

"Because you drank? That's not important. I'm not talking about your drinking. I'm talking about your heart."

He looked up at me to see if I was serious, to see if it was possible that at 49, two days before his death, he could be hearing The Blessing he had been waiting for—unconsciously, fearfully, longingly—his whole life.

Then his eyes teared up too, and, for a second, the pain left his face.

"Father And Son"

When I was coming of age in the Seventies, there was a trio of father-son songs that hooked me every time I heard them on the radio—Harry Chapin's "Cat's in the Cradle," Neil Young's "Old Man," and Cat Stevens's "Father And Son."

With Harry's song, it was the last verse that really hit me, when it's the son now who doesn't have time for the father: "As I hung up the phone it occurred to me/he'd grown up just like me, my boy was just like me."

In Neil's, two spots always stood out. The first is "Old man, take a look at my life/I'm a lot like you were"—that *my* little life could have anything in common with my immense Old Man's was inconceivable until I heard those lyrics. The second was the simple, "Twenty-four and so much more." Here, I felt a son's possibility; a whole new world out there beyond my father's circumspect neighborhood. And this, again, was revelatory: I somehow believed my father's world was the end of the world; that there was nothing beyond his orbit, his force field.

But it was Cat's song that moved me the most deeply. I felt a surge of connection with the Son's first, pained words:

> How can I try to explain,
> 'cause when I do he turns away again,
> It's always been the same, same old story.
> From the moment I could talk
> I was ordered to listen…

His Father has addressed him as "you," but for the distant, hurt, angry Son, it's still "he"—still the same story, still not listening.

And then there's the powerful Father-Son counterpart near the end of the song: the Son feeling compelled to go "Away, away, away" and the Father cautioning him to take it slowly, you're still young—"Stay, stay, stay." A father-son tug-of-war.

It is the Son's voice that prevails:

> If they were right I'd agree
> but it's them they know not me
> now there's a way,
> and I know I have to go away,
> I know I have to go.

I loved the strength of this Son. He understands who he is, and is therefore capable of resisting what "they" deem is right for his life. He knows he has to leave his father's path and find his own way to happiness. To manhood.

Yes, I love the Son's strength at the end—but finally, it's the song's interwoven undertow that stirs my deep sadness. These two voices quietly in love, quietly at war, tugging at each other. Father and Son. Inseparable, irreconcilable.

I want the Father to listen. I want the Son to stay. I want the hurt to heal. I want Blessings all around.

Absent Homer, Lost Bart

And the Emmy for "All-Time Biggest Loser TV Father" goes to...Doh!...Homer Simpson! He is a child, completely obsessed with his own primitive needs: powerless at work, powerless in the world, powerless at home. At the beginning of every episode, he pulls into the driveway—and inevitably ends up with a beer in front of the boob tube.

Homer is an absent father. Technically, physically, he's there—but emotionally, psychologically he's absent, clueless, checked-out.

Unlike Homer, my father was powerful at work, powerful in the world, and powerful at home. His physical presence was unquestionable—but emotionally, psychologically, he, too, was often absent, clueless, and checked-out. He, too, was an absent father.

Which makes Bart and me—and millions of other boys—lost sons. Guy Corneau, in his book *Absent Fathers, Lost Sons*, explains that the sons of absent fathers are not so much lost in some absolute sense, but we have been "lost to the fathers [we] are unconsciously looking for." It's the emotional connection between our fathers and us that is lost.

It has taken me most of my life to understand this. My father's presence was so intense, so immense—he was the provider extraordinaire, spectator at my ball games with the loudest voice, King of the house—there seemed to be absolutely no room for "absence." He was the greatest force in my life; my psyche bent toward him like a plant toward the sun. He was the Great Santini, not homely Homer.

But yes, finally, I was lost. A lost, Unblessed son who craved an emotional-physical-psychological connection with his father. And I think he was lost, too. I'm sure he craved the same connection with his father, and not receiving it, didn't know how to create it with me, his son.

The Simpsons is now in its sixteenth season, and Bart is the exact same boy he was in season one. Given Homer's absence, not surprisingly, he hasn't grown a lick. But there's still hope. I was in my thirty-third season, at least, before I began to grow up.

The Song of Father-Son

Son, I am sorry I was absent. I am sorry I wasn't there for you every time you needed me. I am present now, and I see a son who has all he needs to be a strong, loving man. I see a son who will be the first present father in a long line of loving, present fathers

The City of Lost Sons

I have lived in Detroit for the last fifteen years. I am a white man in a city that is 85% black. Many of the young black men who lived in my old Warrendale neighborhood, and those who live in my present neighborhood in the Cultural Center, and the young black men I occasionally teach at Henry Ford Community College, are being raised my their mothers or grandmothers or aunties; their fathers do not live with them. I am significantly older than these young men; and my father was a fixture in our house. What could I possibly have in common with these young, fatherless, black men?

A whole lot, it turns out.

That's what Helma Massey, one of those Detroit mothers, taught me. She stuck a book in my front door, and the way I look at young black men, and myself, has never been the same. To celebrate my revelation, I wrote the following poem:

The City of Lost Sons
(for Helma Massey)

Black mother reading a book.
I've read a million books.
What are you reading? I asked.

Absent Fathers, Lost Sons.
Interesting, I said.
She said it was. Deeply.

Three days later, the book appeared
in my Detroit front door:
"Dec. 1992. To Peter. New friend."

The Song of Father-Son

I've read it four times since
(and a hundred books on the same topic)
But only today did it occur to me

that I'm in the same family
as the black boys who strut my street:
lost sons in a city of absent fathers.

The World of Unblessed Sons

Growing up, what did you want your father to say to you? What words did you crave from him? What words from him were you dying, literally dying, to hear?

What I wanted my father to say to me was pretty simple.

Son, I'm proud of you.

That's it, that's what I wanted more than anything. And he could have said it anytime—after I brought home yet another "A"; after I scored ten points in a basketball game; after I wrote a poem; after I was nice to my sister.

Son, I'm proud of you.

Or what would have been even better, he could have said it when I hadn't accomplished anything so concrete and worthy. He could have said it first thing in the morning, while I was eating corn flakes at the kitchen table. He could have said it at night, right before he closed my bedroom door. *Son, I'm proud of you.* If he had said it then, it would have meant even more. It would have meant:

Son, you don't have to make the honor roll or the basketball team. You're good enough just as you are. Right now, without accomplishing another thing. You can relax. You're enough.

I didn't know I was enough. If I wasn't doing something important, accomplishing something, achieving something, I felt I was worthless. But I think my father could have reassured me that that wasn't true; he could have convinced me that even if I wasn't working, I was worthy. I think he's the only person in the world who could have convinced me of that.

Son, I'm proud of you. Without changing a thing, you're enough.

If I had heard that growing up—even once, clearly, sincerely, definitively—I think I would have come to believe I wouldn't always be this boy working his ass off so he can feel good about himself, feel strong, feel like a man. I suspect I would have finally come to believe the essential underlying message that only my father could convince me of:

Son, you have all it takes to be a strong, loving man.

This is what I wanted my father to say to me while I was growing up, and I wanted him to hug me when he said it. This is The Blessing. I wanted my father to give me The Blessing.

Son, I'm proud of you. You're enough. You have all it takes to be a strong, loving man.

I suspect you, too, wanted your father to give you The Blessing. Maybe not in exactly the same words, but in the same spirit: *Son, you're OK. You're a man. I love you.* I suspect, like me, you craved his Blessing, would damn near have died for his Blessing—although you might have had to pretend it didn't mean shit to you. And maybe you're still pretending that. Or maybe you've filled the hole opened in you by not getting The Blessing with so many addictions you've forgotten what you originally craved. Or maybe you've never forgotten that—all your life you've been acutely aware of not getting what you wanted from your father—but have had absolutely no idea how to get It.

Welcome to my world. Welcome to the world of most sons. Welcome to the world of Unblessed Sons.

Son, I'm sorry I never said the words you so wanted to hear. They were always here in my heart, and sometimes, oh so many times, they were right there on my lips...I'm sorry for the pain I caused by not finding a way to hug you and to speak them. Let me say them now, let me hug you like you wanted to be hugged, and let me say them to you now: Son, I'm proud of you. You're strong, you're loving, you're a man. I honor all that you are, and all that you are becoming. I am blessed to have you as my son.

WHAT THE BLESSING ISN'T...AND IS

The Lamp

When I was ten, my brother and I each got to pick out a lamp for Christmas. I had selected this fragile porcelain golf ball lamp. It reminded me of one of my heroes, Arnold Palmer. My father, who had radar for future broken things, was skeptical, but consented.

Long story short: An attempted "field goal" with my slipper went awry...the lamp wobbled...I wobbled...the lamp fell, I dove...the lamp cracked on the hardwood floor...and my father charged up the stairs.

He eyed the three or four eggshelled pieces of lamp on the ground. "Were you fooling around?" He didn't say it loudly, but I heard the treble of rage in his words.

"Yes," I said meekly.

He stalked over to the lamp and gripped the base of it like someone strangling the life out of a child. He raised the lamp over his six foot-high head—then brought it smashing to the floor. I flinched, as pieces grenaded everywhere. He raised the lamp—and smash! One more time: smash! Then he dropped the mangled lamp on the floor, slamming the door as he left the room.

I pulled the covers over me and huddled in the dark. It was a long time before I shivered myself to sleep.

The Curse

The Blessing says, *Son, you're enough. You're big enough. You're smart enough. You're loving enough. You don't have to hide who you are. Your emotions, all of them—your sadness, your fear, your anger, your shame, your joy—all of them are welcome here.*

The Curse says, Boy:

—You'll never be enough. You'll always be small, broken, a weakling, a mama's boy, a faggot.

—You'll always be stupid, an idiot, a moron, a shithead.

—You'll always be a loser. Unlovable, unfit for loving. Give it up.

—And you damn well better hide all that cry-baby crap, stuff that fear, I don't want to see your anger, shame on you for feeling shame, and what's so fucking funny?

Sometimes, The Curse is words, sometimes it's just looks. Both are effective. Both say the same thing: You'll never be enough. You'll never be a man.

Sound and feel familiar?

If you didn't get The Blessing, chances are very good you got The Curse. If your father was incapable of giving you The Blessing, he might have been masterful at giving you The Curse.

A father doesn't even have to be there to give you The Curse. My good friend's father left when he was ten. Just his leaving told my friend all he needed to know about himself: I must be a loser, I must be weak, I must have disappointed him. I must not be good enough. If I had been good enough, my father would still be here.

Who got The Curse?

Just about every man now in jail—and every man who believes throwing people in jail is the answer. Just about every boy who kicks cats and curses his mom and spits at the street. Just about every so-called "Bad Boy." Just about every driven "Good Boy," for that matter. Just about every workaholic, alcoholic, sexaholic…

In other words, just about all of us. It's probably about equal to the number of boys who didn't get The Blessing.

Is this an excuse for all us Bad Boys and Good Boys and -Holics of all sorts to keep on with the same thoughts and behavior? No. Finally, it is our own responsibility to get The Blessing and to give The Blessing. In the meantime, it has helped me to realize The Curse is as much about our father's thoughts and behavior as our own: clearly someone Cursed them, too. I believe our fathers wanted to give us The Blessing; but Unblessed themselves, what they most often manifested—tragically for both our sakes—was The Curse.

Son, I wish with all my heart I had had the strength and love to bless you when you were young rather than curse you. If I could do it all over, this is what I would have said to you: You're a beautiful boy. You have all you need to be a strong, loving, beautiful man. I would have said that each and every night, as I closed your bedroom door, and twice on Sundays. I'm saying it to you now: you are a strong, loving, beautiful man.

The Metamorphosis

In my first year of teaching, I happened one day to quote the opening sentence of Kafka's "The Metamorphosis": "Gregor Samsa awoke one fine day and found he was a cockroach."

I told my eleventh-grade boys he was stuck on his beetled-back, in bed, furiously working his numerous legs to right himself and get to work.

They loved it. Every day after that Mike in the back row would clamor, "Hey, Mr. P, tell us about the cockroach, tell us about the guy who turned into a cockroach!"

Twenty years later, I can tell them about a lot of guys who turned into cockroaches. A lot of guys who woke up one horrible day and found themselves flat on their back, unable to get out of bed—boys who metamorphosized into measly insects, instead of into men. Dozens of guys wounded, as Gregor is, by fathers who hurl apples and insults at them to drive them back into their rooms. Hundreds of guys crushed by fathers who are frightened by the sons they see in front of them; by blind fathers who can't see the role they've played in creating these insect-sons. By fathers who Curse their sons instead of Blessing them.

The Curse can transform sons into worms, vermin, predators...

And even cockroaches. A Cursed boy feels like shit, thinks of himself as shit; hides his ugliness all day and feeds ravenously at night on scraps of garbage.

I don't think I ever told those boys what happens to Gregor Samsa—found by the cleaning lady dead in his room, literally starved of love, and his father saying, "Well, thanks be to God." I wanted a miracle for Gregor. I wanted the same miracle for my sixteen-year-old students.

What I wanted, I now realize, was for someone to give them The Blessing.

Boys, listen to me, you are not pieces of shit, you are not cockroaches. Anybody who has told you that, or made you feel that, is full of shit himself. You are lions and dolphins and red-tailed hawks. You will wake up one fine day and find yourselves strong and loving men.

The Fight

If we don't get The Blessing, eventually we will fight for it.

At some point in our lives, even the quietest of us, the peacemakers, the Nice Guys, will strap on gloves and fight for The Blessing. Maybe we'll fight our fathers, our brothers, our bosses, utter strangers in bars—fight to earn The Blessing, like it's some trophy.

It's not a trophy; we can't earn it. We don't have to earn it.

Either we don't know that, or we know it but it doesn't matter. We strap on the gloves. We go down into some dark basement with some other angry men. We fight. We fight for The Blessing.

Terry fights his father every day. They spit words at each other, rip each other up. One day it got physical. Terry was 50, his father 70. But that didn't matter; age doesn't matter. This was Son vs. Father. This fight was 50 years in the making. When a father can only Curse his son, tell him how he's not good enough, not smart enough, not disciplined enough—Not Enough—the fight is on.

I tried to break it up; I tried to step in when I saw Terry punching his father right out there on their small Detroit front lawn on a sun-lit Saturday morning. Terry chased me off; eventually left. His father eventually lost an eye. Now they fight about that, fight about the fight.

I kicked your ass, the son can say. Fair and square. I *must* be a man.

My cousin never beat his father up physically, though he could have. He beats his father up by making a success of himself. He beats his father up, and himself too, by working his ass off sixty hours a week, while his father stayed at home like a bum.

My cousin still beats up his father, even though his father is dead. Death doesn't mean shit to a boy who never got The Blessing.

My father's dead too, and for four or five years after his death, I beat him up in poems.

Petey's "Rocky"

In a dream,
I knock you down
with an angry right.
The referee pulls me
to the same neutral corner
I've been in all my life,
far from you,
then starts the count…

I kicked your ass in poems, in dreams. Fair and square. I *must* be a man.

The President can't beat up on his father, so he finds somebody he can beat up on—and lets the bombs drop.

I kicked your ass with firepower. Fair and square. I *must* be a man.

Nope. Not true. We are all still angry boys begging for The Blessing.

Son, I'm sorry, I'm deeply, deeply sorry. Instead of honoring you, I too often found fault with you. Instead of blessing you, I too often cursed you. I understand your anger—I understand why you want to fight me for your manhood. Let me say this to you now. Let me give you a blessing from the corner: You are a strong, loving man. You don't have to fight me, or anybody else, to prove that. That's in you; strength and love are your birthright. And now let me give you what you have always deserved: a hug, a strong, loving hug. The kind of hug a proud father gives to the powerful, loving man who is his son.

Pass This Test

One of my college roommates had a father who loved IQ tests. First thing he'd do when he met you…give you a puzzle to solve. If you solved it, you were a man; if you didn't, you were a moron.

One of my father's friends loved women. If you could pick up women as easily as you picked up a loaf of bread, you were a man; if you didn't, you were soft.

For some fathers, it's scoring touchdowns. For other fathers, it's sucking back tears at the saddest times.

For most fathers, there's some test sons have to pass. Son, if you pass this test…you're a man. It's usually the same test *their* father gave them.

My father's test was building a security wall around your family. For him, a Depression baby, the world was an unstable place; only a heroic, vigilant effort would keep Evil out of the living room. He worked and worried his ass off to build a castle dead in the middle of suburbia. An extra-safe place to raise his family.

I didn't want a family, and I certainly didn't want anything to do with a security wall. There was this whole wide world out there, and I wanted to explore it. I was the man in Rilke's poem who stands up during supper, goes outside, and keeps on walking…toward the church in the East his father had forgotten.

I failed his test. I was smart, worldly, popular—but I wasn't a man.

But even if I had passed his test and had earned the designation "man," this is not the same as The Blessing. The Blessing is not a test a son passes; not something earned. The Blessing is a recognition by the father of what is already there, in the son.

The Blessing is nothing if it is not unconditional.

Son, you don't have to make $1,000,000 dollars or sleep with 10,000 women or score 20,000 points or have a 200 IQ to be a man. If you have those things or do those things, great. But that's frosting. And know there are people who have accomplished those things and are not, by my account, men. You have all you need right now, all it takes right now, to be a strong, loving man. On your birth day, on the day your head crowned, you became a King.

"You're Gay!"

My wife, Julia, teaches seventh-graders. The harshest curse she hears from these kids, the one packing the most damage, the most shame, hands down?

"You're gay!"

It's the ultimate curse for these twelve-year-old boys because it is The Curse boiled down to two words.

"You're gay!" says, You're not a man. You don't have what it takes. Forget about being a man; you're not even a boy. You're a girl! And somehow it implies you will NEVER be a man. You will NEVER have what it takes.

You are permanently, for the rest of your life, forever...not enough.

Which is exactly how all the boys in her class feel.

If you don't feel like you're man enough, if you're afraid you'll never have what it takes—if no man has Blessed you by saying you are enough—find the boy who looks even more afraid than you are and yell, "You're gay!"

Curse that Unblessed boy. Curse him good. Better him than you, because you know how easily you could be next.

Julia, incredibly patient, has no patience for this. She has told them "You're gay!" and "Faggot!" will not be tolerated in her classroom. She has told them she has good friends of hers, and family members, who are gay and lesbian. She has told them that she believes Gay Rights are the Civil Rights of this generation. And because they respect her, they rarely shout out these Curses anymore. At least not around her.

But, though she wishes it with all her heart, she cannot give her boys The Blessing. Only a man can, an elder, a father. And until Tyrone and Tommy and all the other boys hear it from a man that they have what it takes to be a man, "You're gay!" will never be far from their lips.

Homophobia is the Curse of Unblessed boys.

My Son, gay or straight, you are enough. You are powerful and loving. Let no boy or man convince you of anything different. I love you for the beautiful, strong boy you are, and the beautiful, strong man you will become.

Now That's a Man!

When we don't get The Blessing, when a father doesn't tell us we have all it takes to be a man, we don't know what a man is supposed to be.

All we know for sure is it's not us: We are not-men.

The next logical move is to think: A Man must be the *opposite* of what I am. For me, since I'm wiry and middle-class and book-smart, a "Man" is bulky and working-class and tool-smart. That mechanic with thick hands, that truck driver with beefy forearms, that construction worker with broad shoulders: *That's* a Man!

Funny thing is, that mechanic, that truck driver, that construction worker might well look at me and think I'm The Man because I have a higher education. In my old, working-class Detroit neighborhood, Ramone called me "The Professor." He introduced me to his Puerto Rican family as that: "Meet the Professor!" He was proud of me, proud of that, and, I sensed, ashamed that he had only graduated high school.

Meanwhile, all I wanted to be was "one of the guys," like Ramone.

So many of us are not-men who think that our alleged opposites *are* Men. And we are filled with shame.

When we are Blessed, we are all Men. And the shame dissolves.

Son, you have everything you need to be a man in this world. That man over there who seems like a real Man to you…who knows? I hope he is. I hope he feels the love and the power inside him. I hope you do, too. I pray you never forget all the love and strength inside of you—that you are the kind of man that others see and say, Now that's a man!

Stoney & Wojo

Lately, I've found myself listening to sports talk with "Stoney and Wojo."

Talking sports, listening to sports, watching sports soothes me. I used to watch sports—from football to golf—with my father. He sat in his leather throne, I sat on the couch as close to him as I could get. The Zenith blared away from across the room. I don't remember us talking very much, mostly watching. All Sunday afternoon until the family room was consumed by shadows.

Was this sports watching The Blessing?

No. But it was the best I could do. It was as close as I could get to my father.

Most days, Stoney and Wojo are annoyingly amusing, at best. They play silly games, make crude comments, and occasionally shame callers. They are clearly 40-year-old boys.

But hearing them, I remember my father and me on Sunday afternoons, sports filling up that family room, connecting us.

For me, and probably for Stoney and Wojo and most of their callers, listening to sports, watching sports, talking about sports, playing sports was as close as we ever got to our fathers. As close as we ever got to The Blessing.

So no wonder Stoney & Wojo keep talking and I keep listening. When we talk sports, our fathers appear. And maybe this time, they will turn in their leather thrones, look in our eyes, and Bless us.

Son, it's not just sports that makes me feel connected to you. We can talk about more than batting averages and won-lost records; we can talk about what's going on in your life—your own wins and injuries, your game plans and your trades, your joy and your anger. I am the biggest fan of the strong, loving man you already are.

Our Father Who Art in Heaven

I've been searching all of my life for a father to give me The Blessing. Any father strong enough and loving enough to tell me I was man enough, just as I was.

I've gravitated toward several father figures, men who crossed my path at a certain time who were full of love for what they were doing and wisdom about how to do—one was a teacher, one was a revolutionary. They gave me what they could, which was a lot, and I went away less hungry.

When I was twenty, I found the ultimate father figure, God himself. Our Father. My Father for about a year.

It was a wonderful year. I was full of strength, love, certainty. I was down right righteous (and not for the last time in my life). I had finally found a Father big enough to fill my hole. You are my Son, he said to me, whom I love; with you I am well pleased. It was a parentage made in Heaven. From my baptism, this Father had been in my life, in my prayers: "Our Father who art in heaven…" His son had hung in front of St. Helen's church in Schenectady and the little church in Galway, in churches everywhere, crucified, on his way home to his Father.

Now, finally, He was my Father too.

So why didn't it last? Why, after little more than a year, did He abandon me? Why did He leave me hanging? My God, my God, why hast thou forsaken me?

Twenty-five years later, I still don't know for sure. Maybe He was just too abstract for me—He couldn't deliver on the physical part of The Blessing—He couldn't hug me, touch me, look me in the eyes. And His words lost their Blessing power. I desperately wanted Him to be the father that would heal me, Bless me. Given my situation, He was the logical, inevitable, all-powerful choice.

I have family, friends, and students who do feel Blessed by Him, sons who have finally found their loving, powerful, heavenly Father. I wish them peace.

But I cannot lie to myself on this all-important matter. I no longer felt Blessed by Him. As simple, and painful, as that. My search for The Blessing, for the father who could give me The Blessing, resumed.

Sometimes I Feel like a Fatherless Child

A decade ago I wrote a book of poems called "Rhonda's Talk Show." Rhonda was everything I wasn't—black, working-class, female. What we did share was a hard-working, disappearing father.

Rhonda Ironing

Your dark blue work pants stretched tight
    on the ironing board.

Your daddy wore the same dark blue pants
    to the factory—
neatly creased when he walked out the door
    each day at dawn.
On weekends, he didn't look right
    in jeans or sweats.
He died in those blue work pants—
    heart attack,
    two years short of 30-and-out
    one week short of your tenth birthday.
At the funeral, he didn't look right
    lying there in fancy black pants
    and an old, tired face.

> *When you started,*
> > *your supervisor had to write you up*
> > > *three times*
> *before you'd wear blue work pants.*
>
> *Tonight, you iron them with*
> *short, hard strokes—*
> *the wrinkles*
> *disappearing*
> *like the lines on*
> *your father's*
>
> *face*

What, exactly, has disappeared at the end—her father's wrinkles or her father's face? Can she see him young again, vibrant—or is he fading…fading from her life? Is he vivid enough to still bless her—or is she totally on her own, all blessings done?

I don't know.

Sometimes I feel like a fatherless child a long, long ways from home. Other times I feel like my own father who is finally coming home.

David

Michelangelo knew something about The Blessing. A lot of artists do, maybe because they didn't get The Blessing. Maybe because their art comes right out of the center of the wound opened up from not getting The Blessing.

Michelangelo said he didn't create David. David was already there, in the marble. He just chopped away the excess.

That's what The Blessing does. The Blessing recognizes what is right there, the essence beneath the excess. The Blessing chops away all the doubts and fears and masks—all the cold marble—to the strong, splendorous man inside.

Unconditional Love

What's that?

It really doesn't compute with me: unconditional love? As in, you don't have to earn it, you don't have to do anything, anything at all, to deserve it? You're loved simply because you're here on this planet, planted in front of your TV set on a Sunday afternoon watching the Lions?

That's impossible. Too good to be true. Absurd. Ridiculous.

In fact, it makes me angry. I've been working my ass off all my life to be a better person—a person worthy of love. I read Dale Carnegie's *How to Win Friends and Influence People* when I was ten; I read Norman Vincent Peale's *The Power of Positive Thinking* when I was eleven; I read Thomas a Kempis' *The Imitation of Christ* when I was twelve; and I've read just about every self-help book written since, from Dyer to Covey.

Almost every day of the last thirty years, I've gotten up and got at it again, pecking away at my ultimate Project: to turn myself into a man who is loving and worthy of love.

So don't even talk to me about unconditional love!

What happened? What happened to me that the most beautiful idea in the world—that someone could be loved just for who they are—an idea I instantly understand when I think of my cat, Huey—could seem so patently impossible when applied to me?

I'll tell you what happened. I never got The Blessing.

The Blessing is, by definition, a proclamation of unconditional love. It is the concrete form unconditional love can take between a father and a son. And because The Blessing is that, The Blessing can help free a man from the shackles of endless self-improvement.

Son, you have all it takes to be a strong, loving man. Right now, right here, right inside of you. Go climb Everest, if you want, make a million dollars, read a thousand self-help books. Do all that, if you want. But if you don't do any of it, you are still enough. Regardless of what you do, or don't do, I will love you...today, tomorrow, always.

Enough, Now

Lately, I've noticed how many of my thoughts are future-focused. In my head, I'm nearly always *preparing* to do something, to say something, to solve something. And when I'm not tripping forward, I'm often stumbling backward and evaluating how I did something, said something, tried to solve something yesterday.

I don't spend much time right here, right now. Something deep inside of me doesn't trust right here, right now. Something deep inside me says, There's not enough right here, right now; *you're* not enough right here, right now.

I've believed in my not-enoughness and the world's not-enoughness as far back as I can remember.

My father was a tremendous sprinter; a pigeon-toed speedster—a guy fast enough to out-run has past for sixty-three years. He threw himself into the future, eyes straight-ahead, body and mind churning like there was only tomorrow. The past—with all its heavy Depression and death and Unblessing—was the Boogeyman running him down in his dreams. Right here, right now was not a safe place to be; farther down the road was better, safer. Farther down the road of accomplishment was a place called Enough. My father was an Unblessed boy running for his life.

The Blessing helps anchor a man in the here, the now, the enough.

Son, you can stop running now. I ran until I dropped, but you don't have to. At least slow down; breathe. There, that's better. Feel your power, feel all the love stored deep inside of you. Feel how right here, right now, you're enough.

Christmas Lights

A boy without The Blessing is like a Detroit house in December: sad windows, indifferent porches, angry locked doors.
　　Then the father flicks on the Christmas lights.

Marathon Man

In my first semester of college two Smith women told me I looked like Dustin Hoffman. I didn't care that he had a big nose or didn't look anything at all like Robert Redford. *Marathon Man* had just come out. Hoffman was fit, intense, famous—and he had slept with Anne Bancroft.

I danced around their car screaming, "I look like Dustin Hoffman! I look like Dustin Hoffman!" until, frightened, they drove off.

Coming when it did in that first, awkward Amherst semester where I was surrounded by a lot of young men who *did* look like Robert Redford, it was a blessing.

Twenty seven-years later, Dearborn, Michigan. I'm getting my pre-Christmas haircut in Veronica's Hair Salon when I pick up *GQ* and a 67-year-old Dustin blesses me again, directly this time.

In an interview, he's talking about working with an ailing Laurence Olivier in *Marathon Man*:

> *But this is what I'll never forget: After, we went to dinner. And it's etched in my memory when his son came to meet us there, the way he greeted his father: He bent down and kissed his father's head. I'd never seen anybody do that before. I'd never seen a son do that before. He just took his father's delicate head, and he kissed it [wells up]*

I welled up too. While Veronica's daughter played "Simon Says" and Rudy came in with a Christmas bottle of wine, I felt the tears rise up—"his father's *delicate* head"—and surround my eyes.

The end of the interview returns to this moment:

> ***The story about Olivier with his son...***
> Yes.
> ***It was a very moving scene. The way his son greeted him in that restaurant.***
> Now you're onto something.
> ***It must have resonated with you.***
> Of course it did. It was the hard part.
> ***What was the hard part?***
> That part of the relationship I wanted from my father...
> ***The hug?***
> All of it.
> ***The embrace?***
> All of it.
> ***Not just the physical embrace, the emotional embrace.***
> All of it. And the last thing I did to my father as he lay dead, I kissed him on his head. [fights back tears]

Sitting there waiting for a haircut, three days before my sixth Christmas without my father, I too had to fight back tears.

I remembered a poem I had written:

> Good Night, Father
>
> I don't remember a single hug.
> A few sentences of praise.
> One letter.
>
> But I kissed your rough right cheek
>   good night
>   every night
> and on the day you died.

What do we sons want from our fathers?

All of it.

All. Of. It.

And we won't stop running until we get It.

Man Enough

You mean, I don't have to be more than this? I don't have to puff myself up each morning before I go out of the house? I don't have to make more, lift more, screw more, win more?

You're saying I'm man enough right now, as I am? You're saying I can stop trying so hard, that I can relax? Is that what you're telling me? You want me to believe that, you think I can believe that?

Have you looked at my bank account—have you looked at my body? I'm not rich enough—I'm not strong enough. Have you looked at my secretary? Now, if I could nail her…

You mean, I'm man enough right now, as I am? You're saying I can stop trying so hard, that I can relax? Is that what you're telling me? You want me to believe that bullshit, you think I can believe that bullshit?

You think just because you say it, it's suddenly going to be true? Do you know how long I've felt like this, do you no how long I've felt this fucking small, this fucking weak?

And don't even talk to me about fathers and their god damn Blessing.

Have you met my father? Me either. He was a punk. He left when I was two, ten, twenty.

Have you met my father? Too bad. He was an asshole. He beat me when I was two, ten, twenty.

Have you met my father? Maybe. He was invisible. I didn't see him, he didn't see me…when I was two, ten, twenty.

Have you met my father? Hell yes. He was a man's man. He was more of a man at two, ten, twenty than I'll ever be…

You mean, I'm man enough right now, as I am? You're saying I can stop trying so hard, that I can relax? Is that what you're telling me? You want me to believe that, you think I can actually believe that?

Who the hell are you, anyway?

Son, I am the father you never had giving you The Blessing you never got. I am the father you've been searching so long for. I am the man telling you you can stop trying

39

so hard to prove you're a man; that yes, you can relax. I am the man telling you that, right now, you are strong enough, loving enough...man enough.

My Blessing

Dad, how fucking hard would it have been to hug my skinny, driven body to yours and tell me I was OK? That I was doing enough; I had what it takes; I could rest? It didn't have to be every day. It didn't have to be every week. It didn't even have to be every year. It didn't have to be when I was twelve or thirteen when I most confused about all this manhood stuff; it could have been later. It could have been any time, any fucking time, before you died. Anytime before I was going on 39 and you were dead at 63.

Son, I wanted to. Oh how I wanted to. When you were a boy and I'd close your door every night…then, then, if I had the words. If I had the courage. If I had the skills. If I could have slowed down myself. If, if, if…. Forgive me. Can you forgive me? Can you accept what I see so clearly now and can finally say? I can tell you from the bottom of my heart you're doing enough; you have all it takes; you're a beautiful, powerful, loving man. You can rest, of course you can rest. Please rest. And may my Blessing be the last thing you hear tonight, and each night, for the rest of your life: I'm proud of the son you were, the man you are, and the father you will be. Sweet dreams, my son.

Being Heard

I admit it. These days, when I feel I'm not being heard, I'll sometimes throw a teenage temper tantrum. A volcanic hissy-fit. I will shout so loud it even scares me—**"YOU'RE NOT LISTENING TO ME!!!!"**—jackknifing the air the whole time with an index finger aimed at someone's jugular.

I even had a therapist who I had to tell to SHUT UP! I'M PAYING YOU—LET ME TALK!

It's not pretty. I'm not entirely proud of it. But, believe it or not, it's progress.

As a child, I never felt listened to. Not deeply, anyway. Nobody took the time and the energy to hear my pain, to sit with my anger and my fear, to welcome my sadness and my shame, and to share my joy. My father was too distracted, too disconnected from and uncomfortable with his own emotions to pull off anything like that; the best he could offer was his own well intentioned, thoroughly subjective advice—which, being a Good Son, I swallowed obediently. My mother had more of a clue here, but she was too tangled in her own guilt and sadness to hear the depths of mine.

The greatest tragedy of not being deeply heard as a child was the conclusion I somehow drew that I did not have the right, or even the need, to be deeply heard. I was fine—other people were the ones in pain, and it was my duty to listen to them, to hear their pain. Repressing my own need to be heard, I became a wonderful listener. I did unto others what I unconsciously wanted others to do unto me. I listened deeply to my father, I listened deeply to my mother, I listened deeply to friends, girl friends and complete strangers...

And I'm at a point now in my life where all the suppressed, repressed anger at NOT being heard when I've heard so much occasionally roars out. IT'S MY TURN NOW, GOD DAMMIT! I'VE DONE A WORLD OF LISTENING TO YOUR PAIN—LISTEN TO MY PAIN NOW! Having played the Rescuer until I felt the anger of the Victim, I'm in full-blown Persecutor. So watch the fuck out!

Although part of me relishes my 30-years-overdue coming-of-age tantrums, and understands it's got to be ugly before it gets pretty, I also realize my **Hear me!** explosions don't get me heard. I am finding the concrete ways to ask for the kind of deep listening I periodically need in my life: "I would like you to mirror the emotions running through me; I would like for you to ask, 'Is there more?' before you jump in with your thoughts, feelings, or advice."

That's all I've ever wanted—to be truly and deeply heard. I believe that's a huge, deep want of every person on this planet. It's the spirit of The Blessing. The Blessing isn't, finally, about saying the perfect words or giving the perfect advice. The Blessing is about a father being open and present for his son. The Blessing is being heard.

Son, tell me what's going on in your in your life and in your heart. Tell me all of it, if you want. You are my son, and I welcome it all.

In a Nutshell

The Blessing is more than a generalized, positive affirmation. More than "That's great, Son. You're great. I love you."

At the very least—and it's a ton—The Blessing blesses a boy's body and a boy's emotions. These are two fragile areas for a lot of fathers. I know very few men who are comfortable with their bodies, and even fewer men who are comfortable expressing the full range of their emotions.

My father lived in a tight little box. He had a beautiful, powerful body, but I sense he was ashamed of it, afraid of it somehow. And no surprise, afraid of hugging. He was also afraid to show his fear, his sadness, and his shame. Although he was a quick-witted, funny man, and I sometimes saw him laugh, his joy also felt smothered. Most days, he emitted a restless anxiousness that occasionally erupted into anger.

He passed on his tight little box to me.

The Blessing tells a boy—or a man—his body is OK as it is, and his emotions, all of them, are welcome.

Son [hugging him], I am here to tell you you have a strong body and a big heart. Maybe you feel small today. Do you? Don't worry; your bones and your muscles and your penis, all of them will grow. You have all you need to be a strong man. And a loving man, too. A loving man feels a lot of things: he feels sad sometimes, mad sometimes, happy sometimes, fearful sometimes, ashamed sometimes. I feel all of those things just about every day. And so do you, right? And each one of those feelings is OK. Your sadness, your anger, your fear, your happiness, your shame—they're all welcome in this house. Everything about you—your body, your emotions, your thoughts—is welcome in this house. You're my strong, loving son who will grow into a strong, loving man. You're great just the way you are. And I love you.

BLESSING OUR EMOTIONS

A Man's Best Friend

I grew up with dogs—dogs in the house, dogs in the pens behind the house. Golden retrievers (Bull, Gunner), Gordon setters (BB), Britney spaniels (Duke), German shorthaired pointers (Coco, Angel, Moose)...My mother tolerated them; my father loved them. Dogs were my father's best friend.

After dinner, my father would get down on the family room floor and take care of them. With his white T-shirted back up against his leather chair, he'd cradle them close and clip their toenails or hug them tight and rummage around in their ears with a Q-tip. Sometimes they yelped and bled; sometimes they wiggled their head and crooned. He was somehow gentle and professional at the same time; loving and strong. After completing the necessary clipping/cleaning, he'd get down on all fours and roughhouse with them. He'd rub Coco's belly until she purred or he'd smack and stroke Gunner until he sang or barked or slapped his tail. My father would purr or sing or bark or slap back—igniting more squealy delight from the dogs.

I watched from the couch, loving those moments—my father happy, the dogs happier, the house a-thump with the sounds of life and love.

I should say, most of me loved those moments. When I think back now, I feel an almost overwhelming sadness. I loved those dogs too—but at those moments, when my father was obviously giving them so much attention and getting so much happiness from them, I think a deep part of me wanted to be those dogs. I wanted to be the one cradled and hugged; I wanted my nails and ears to be attended to. I wanted to be the one down on the family room floor roughhousing with my father, squealing with kiddy-giddy happiness.

I wanted to be my father's best friend.

For whatever psychological reason, my father was much better at being physically affectionate and emotionally present with his dogs than with his children. I am sorry that was the case, sorry for me, and sorry for him. But despite the sadness, and some anger, I am still glad to have been a witness to those joyous romps on the family room floor, my father up to his ears in dogs, his own sadness and anger temporarily lost in play.

Years later, I would inherit my grandfather's golden retriever, Windy. Windy had been a gift of solace from my father to his father after my grandmother had died. This dog instantly became a direct, deep connection from me—to my father—and to my father's father.

For the next ten years, Windy followed me everywhere—from my first teaching position in Massachusetts, to grad school in Ann Arbor, to my first home in Detroit. He was everything a dog should be: loyal, loving, forgiving, funny.

I remember calling my dad up to tell him Windy had died. I started crying; I don't remember ever crying in front of my father. He was great. He said it was OK to cry. Windy was a great dog. There was even a catch in his own voice, and maybe, though I'm not sure, tears on the other end of the phone. This was a grief he not only felt, but also felt comfortable enough to allow, to express, to encourage; and I'm grateful for that. And I think we both understood we were mourning more than a wonderful dog's passing. We were mourning the loss of a dear friend. We were mourning the loss of my grandfather, his father, and maybe, too, the loss of my father back on the family room floor many years before.

For a moment, my father and I were each other's best friend.

Mad, Sad, Glad, Fear, Shame

I had read thousands of books. I had written a novel, a screenplay, hundreds of poems, a Master's thesis on Melville.

But I was *emotionally* illiterate.

"What are you feeling?"

When I was asked that, usually by a woman, words, usually my best friends in the world, would flee. A great abyss of silence would open up. Vast grayness.

"I don't know. OK, I guess."

Then, at 42, I went on the Mankind Project's New Warrior Training Adventure weekend.

"What are you feeling?" asked this guy wearing sweats and built like a linebacker. Looking at him, I would have expected a different kind of question—maybe, "How much can you bench press?"

"I don't know. I'm feeling good."

"'Good' isn't a feeling," he said. "Mad, sad, glad, fear or shame?" he asked, ticking each one off on a thick finger. "Pick one."

I couldn't, at first. It took me a minute. I ran through each one on my own fingers—mad, sad, glad, fear, shame—trying them out. I was getting a little frustrated—was "frustrated" a feeling? I looked at the guy, expecting him to be showing signs of one of the many impatient coaches I had played for, the impatient father I had grown up with: Will you hurry up already, for chrissake? Men who didn't have time for feelings. But he was just standing there calmly, arms behind his back, giving me the time to get out of my head and feel whatever it was I was feeling. I ticked them off on my fingers again, slowly this time: mad? sad? glad? fear? shame?

"Sad," I finally said. "I'm feeling sad." And I suddenly felt the tears forming in my eyes, my body telling me I had picked correctly.

"Good," he said. "Your sadness is welcome here."

Hearing that for the first time in my life—your sadness is welcome here—released the tears. I felt them rush down my face without feeling a drop of shame.

One of the underlying messages of The Blessing is that our emotions are welcome. All of them, including shame. I've learned that over the last four years, although I sometimes still need to touch base with my fingers to see what I'm feeling at any given moment.

Son, you are a strong man. Strong enough to cry, strong enough to feel fear and anger and shame, strong enough to speak your joy. I honor your sadness, I honor your fear, I honor your anger, I honor your shame, and I honor your joy. All your emotions are welcome in this house.

Pitch-and-Catch

Several years ago, when I showed Judith, my Jungian therapist, a wallet picture of my father, she looked at it briefly and said, "He looks like a sad man." Up until then, when I looked at the same photo, I saw only a dark, handsome man of twenty-four—chiseled cheekbones, brilliantined black hair—eight months shy of becoming my father.

Was he really sad?

I went home and looked at the collage of pictures I have of him. Not a trace of teeth in any of them—his lips sealed straight across his face as if he were trying to keep something in. Only his eyes held a whisper of smile.

How sad was he?

By this time, through therapy, dreams, and my men's group, I was much more in touch with my own persistent sadness. In fact, I was to the point of getting downright angry at how often I felt sad—a healthy sign. What I had not yet considered, however, was how much of *his* sadness I carried around with me.

While staffing a New Warrior weekend last spring, I got a real gift from a young man who suddenly realized he was walking around with a whole sack of his father's sadness. Inspired, I came home and wrote a poem that starts:

> My father and I play pitch-and-catch
>   with his sadness
> fat as a softball
> hard as a baseball
> back & forth, back & forth.

And I suspect this sadness has been accumulating for generations, passed on from father to son, from father to son, as tenacious as eye color or high cheekbones. I am only the latest reservoir.

What will it take to make my fathers' sadness evaporate? Will I be able to break this sad cycle and spare my son?

Son, your sadness is welcome here. And so is your anger, your fear, your shame, and your joy. Let's play pitch-and-catch with all of them. And let's celebrate the fact you have all you need to be a powerful, gentle, joyful man.

American Men's Lives

That was the name of the course I took, "American Men's Lives." It was 1979, and I was a boy away from home for his second year of college. I was living in a fraternity with a lot of other boys. What did I know about *men's* lives, American or otherwise?

The course was taught by Professor Townsend. If he was your typical American man, I was in trouble: curly black writer's hair, hockey body, Rhodes Scholar. And his first name was "Kim," which I took to mean he was sensitive, too. The guy had it all. And yet I sensed he was struggling as a man, working, searching.

And I remember struggling myself in that course. Whatever it was that he wanted us to see, or wanted to find for himself as an American male, was just out of my reach. I somehow knew this topic was vital to me, knew the second I saw the course title I would take it, but I never felt the click, the revelation. It turned out to be a lot like my intro chemistry class from freshman year where I never really grasped the material but ground-out a "B."

Twenty-five years later, I can't remember a single thing we read that semester. I do remember a key concept, androgyny, and I recall being comfortable with the idea of a male developing his feminine side. Maybe because I was already what Robert Bly calls a "soft male"—a sensitive man in need of some Wild Man masculinity.

And my most vivid memory of Kim Townsend is not from that class. It is from two years later, my senior year, when he gave a moving tribute to a female colleague of his, a young mother, Liz Bruss, who had died suddenly, tragically. Instead of his usual jeans and flannel shirt, Kim was in a dark suit, and his soft, warm words filled up Johnson Chapel. I remember he was crying, as I was, by the end of it.

There we were, two Unblessed American men. Crying. It felt like some big-as-life Final Exam, and it felt like we both aced it.

Recipe to Make a Man Cry

1. Bring him to a circle of men.
2. Have him pick a man to play his father.
3. Have that man, his father, look him in the eyes and tell him, "Son, I'm proud of you."
4. Repeat, "Son, I'm proud of you" until, after maybe fierce silence and nervous laughter, after, perhaps, anger, and then shame…the tears break.

Tears of sadness—because his father never said it.

Tears of joy—because that's all the ever wanted to hear…and now he has.

Johnny Carson

Ed McMahon's deep, friendly-drunk voice—"Heeeeeeeeere's Johnny!" The rousing theme music: Ba! Ba! Ba! Ba!...Ba! BaDa DaDaDa!

Every week night, even before I could stay up to watch it, the upbeat sounds of the "Tonight Show" carried from behind my parents' closed door...down the hall...and into my bedroom. I imagined Johnny tentatively emerging from behind the curtain: flushed face, modest smile, chest peacocked out to display a brilliant red or green or yellow blazer. I imagined my dad settling in for the night—slipping off his watch, dumping spare change into a cookie jar, setting his billfold on the bedroom dresser—while he watched Carson's monologue on their small color TV. I imagined him smiling—unlike McMahon's hearty guffaws, my dad rarely made a sound when he laughed—but I could imagine him smiling when a Carson joke bombed and Johnny did his crestfallen-kid-deadpan straight into the camera.

The "Tonight Show" was my bedtime story, and Johnny Carson was the story's hero. I loved how he and Ed bantered back and forth, laughed, Karnacked each other, enjoyed each other's company. I had seen my father and his best friend, Howard, barb and bullshit back and forth; I learned again this is what men did who liked each other. I loved how gracious Johnny was, how, most nights, with most guests, he'd lean forward and really listen to what people were saying and respond authentically—usually with compassionate humor. I loved how Jim's animals would always scare the hell out of Johnny—bark at him, bite him, barf on him—and Johnny would slapstick-lurch or launch himself like a little boy into Ed's open arms.

But mostly I loved Johnny because my dad seemed to love him. And because, even back then, I somehow sensed that Johnny and my dad had a lot in common. They were both handsome men in an Old School way, with good hair and full faces and fit bodies; men who looked great in colorful blazers and crisp slacks. Successful men from Nowhere, Nebraska and can-you-spell "S-c-h-e-n-e-c-t-a-d-y," New York. They were both brilliantly, off-the-cuff funny—and by their own admission, incredibly shy. They would entertain, and then go hide. Beneath their wit and charm and good looks was a subterranean sadness.

I heard one of Johnny Carson's best friends say that Johnny was so intensely shy and private, so guarded, somebody must have hurt him real badly. Something similar must have happened to my dad, and I feel a tender sadness in saying that.

A Man's Anger

My father's anger filled up the house; there was no room for my own.

My father's anger was so incontestable that he rarely had to unleash it. Early on, he had more than established himself as the Minister of Right and Wrong by whacking us with a board for our bad behavior. Plus, he was six foot tall, a well-developed 185 pounds, with the deepest of voices. When we misbehaved, he no longer needed the board, or even to yell; he just pointed, and we, without a single word, marched up to our rooms.

To challenge him, to show even a hint of anger, was to invite death. Or so my brother and I truly and deeply believed.

Even upstairs, in my own room, it didn't feel safe, or right, to get angry. Good Boys weren't supposed to get angry; Christian boys were supposed to turn the other cheek. Do unto others/Be Polite was my First Commandment.

So not surprisingly, I buried my anger deep in my body. I stuffed it, as Robert Bly would say, into my Shadow Bag. I've come to realize I had no choice about this. Not then anyway. It was something I sensed I had to do in order to survive, first of all, and to remain a Good Boy.

Thirty years go by. Most of those years, the anger stayed deep, deep in the Bag. I was the Good Boy, the Nice Guy, Pete Nice. On rare occasions a chunk leaked out: I punched a lamp, punched my steering wheel. For eight years, I channeled some of that anger into righteous, political rage. Still, most of the anger sat in my stomach like a hand grenade.

Most men I know are incredibly angry. Some show it: they yell, they fight, they bully. Some drown it in beer or wallpaper over it with religion or politics or academics. Some perform a passive-aggressive two-step. Some dodge it, some deny it. Some swallow it, and swallow it, and swallow it for years—until it vomits back up.

And here's the tricky thing: Of the five fundamental emotions—sadness, fear, shame, joy, and anger—anger is the only one permitted to men. Cry, admit you're afraid, own your shame, express your joy? Are you fucking kidding me! But show your anger—yell, curse, fight? OK. That's acceptable for men...up to a point. Then anger becomes *all* of what men are: savages, beasts, monsters.

We men have so few places to go where we can safely express our anger. Sports? For some, for a while. Fight Club? Nonexistent, but I relished the idea of such a place, felt it right in my gut and groin and fists like millions of other men who saw the movie.

For me, my men's group has been that safe place. In Joseph's basement on Monday night, we eight men create a container strong enough and safe enough to hold our anger. A half-dozen times over the last couple of years, my Good Boy, my Nice Guy, has felt safe enough to step out of the way, relinquish control, and let some of that deep buried anger bubble out. I've screamed, kicked, and cursed at stand-in fathers and mothers and coaches. I've attacked pillows with a baseball bat—turned that same bat on a punching bag—and felt the joy of released rage. And I've seen other men do the same.

I should mention that in our first year together, our anger rarely surfaced. It was the red elephant in the basement. Sadness was welcome, fear was welcome, joy was welcome, even shame was welcome. But anger...anger was scary. We intuitively knew that our anger was actually rage—after thirty years in a Shadow Bag, anger alchemizes into rage. And rage would shatter our container into a million pieces. Or so we believed. Just like I believed my father would kill me if I showed any anger. We needed time, trust.

The Blessing acknowledges, accepts, and honors anger without glorifying it. And in so doing, it short-circuits rage.

Son, I know you have a lot of anger in you. Me too, and that's OK. You don't have to bury it; you don't have to blow up buildings with it. Through your anger you can find your Warrior—that part of you that is decisive and strong. Instead of imploding or exploding, instead of beating up yourself or beating up others, instead of internal or external war, you can utilize your anger-turned-strength to build a life of love and peace. Your anger is welcome here.

Men's Rage

Never underestimate a man's rage.

Today, Oprah interviewed a pastor who had brutally beaten his wife with a marble rolling pin and ultimately strangled her with a car seat belt. This was not a man who had any history of violence. Just the opposite: he was the person helping victims of violence. He talked about having an image to uphold; as the community's pastor, he always had to be up, to lift, to assist. And he was also depressed, and now understands all too terribly that depression is anger turned inward. I'm horrified by his crime, but I also see all too clearly where that anger-turned-rotten—that rage—came from.

Very, very few people know the rage in me. Most—my students, my colleagues, my neighbors, many of my friends, much of my family—see me as a thoughtful, even-tempered, kind-hearted man. I've kept the rage hidden from them for decades. I kept the rage hidden from myself for almost as long.

Never underestimate a man's rage.

If his father or mother or someone early in his life abused him—physically, emotionally, sexually—and thereby shamed him, if he has not dealt with that abuse and shame, sought therapy of some kind, pursued healing...rage is inevitable. It's obvious in the bully—hidden in the rescuer; readily apparent in the Bad Boy—latent in the Good Boy; it may appear as sadistic—or masochistic. In any case, the rage is there. A tank of rage, toxic as Agent Orange, that grows and leaks and sometimes explodes.

I remember doing some therapeutic work where I felt so much rage clutched up inside me I was absolutely terrified of opening my mouth. I was sure the yell that blasted out of me would be so soul-shattering loud and vicious that every other man on this men's retreat would hear it and instantly consider me a completely broken, unfixable animal. So rather than feeling the shame of their judgment, I stuffed my rage. Again. Which is the sure-fire way to breed more rage.

"Did something snap?" That's what Oprah wanted to know, and that's the way we often talk about a man's rage. "Something snapped; he just lost it." If a man's been hurt badly—shamed—rage is often the weapon of choice to prevent experiencing shame again. Or the response when he is shamed again.

If you touch a man's shame, he might collapse into silence…or snap into rage. If you shame him deeply enough, he will have to destroy himself—or destroy you.

What are we going to do, we men, with all this rage dynamited up inside of us? Where can we go to express it, and to whom? And how, how the hell are we going to express it? Through violent movies, violent sports, violent video games, violent wars—are those the best, most healing things we can do?

At some point, maybe two years after my father's death, I began taking a leaded baseball bat down into my Detroit basement and beating the shit out of an old couch. I screamed at him, I cursed him, all the while beating the dust-infested couch until I had blisters on my hands and sweat running like whiplashes down my back.

That was a start.

But a man's rage must be witnessed by other men, I believe. It takes other men to confirm I am not a freak for feeling such rage; other men to feel it and express it themselves. Openly, safely.

I've taken my bat to my men's meeting in Joseph's basement. I've screamed loud enough down there to kill ghosts; in that space, in front of a circle of men, I've fought my long-dead father.

And rather than stuffing my anger as I have all my life, and thereby adding to my tank of rage, I've also done "Clearings" in that basement with men I was angry with: Gave them my *Data, Feelings, Judgments,* and *Wants* surrounding their behavior, heard them mirror all that back to me so I felt heard—and then voiced my *Ownership*: laid claim to the stuff *in me* that were the deeper, truer reasons for my anger. Often these Clearings have been emotionally intense, with anger, fear, shame, sadness banging off the walls; sometimes men are pissed enough to shout their judgments and their wants. But not once has any man been physically touched, and these Clearings more often than not end with hugs and genuine joy. A big piece of that joy comes from men recognizing it's OK to be angry, and that there are safe places and safe processes where a man can express his anger.

The Blessing derails rage because it honors a son's anger and insulates a son from shame.

Son, your rage is welcome here. Show it, speak it, and I will do my best to hear it. I also want to tell you that you have all you need, everything, all the strength and love and beauty, to be a man. You are enough, right now, just as you are. When someone triggers your shame and you feel your rage rising, remember this: you lack nothing, you're enough. I am proud of your power and your love.

Surprised by Joy

I wake up almost every morning with sadness circling my eyes and fear hovering in my gut; I've got a reservoir of anger ready to geyser and a tank full of toxic shame leaking all over. But joy, the fifth basic emotion—where the hell is that? Where is it in my body, where is it in my life?

It seems I can go years without feeling joy. And when it does come, it's a flicker, a flash, a fluke second—gone.

My friend Jimmy had a splendid moment of joy the other day. He's hyper-punctual like I am, and he had told his wife he'd be home at 5:30. He was already a couple of minutes late as he swung the car into the driveway—just as this song came on the radio, a song he heard maybe ten times the last week, a song he immediately liked but hadn't paid any real attention to. If he listened to it now, he'd be even later; his wife, seven-and-a-half months pregnant, might need him; her needs were certainly more important than his needs, her time more important than his time…He'd had to make this decision thousands and thousands of times before in life, starting with his mother's needs thirty-five years ago. It was a no-brainer: he was fine, he was OK, it was just a song…*they* were in more pain, *their* needs were more important.

But on this day, he pulled his foot back into the car, closed the door, closed his eyes, and for the next three minutes, listened, really listened, to this beautiful song.

"When I got out of the car," he said, "I felt this…joy. I barely know what joy feels like because I've got like this blanket of sadness all the time. But this was it, this was joy. It must be more complicated, but I just took care of my own needs for three minutes—and there it was."

Maybe for some it's not more complicated than that. I know men have the rap of being selfish, of *only* taking care of their own wants and needs; and I've seen men who I judged that was true for. But I also know many men, myself and Jimmy included, who from a very early age have taken on the duty of satisfying the wants and needs of others, often at the expense of our own wants and needs. For complex reasons, we took on the role of rescuers or protectors or problem-solvers. Joy was something we could make happen for others; it was selfish, we were taught and came to believe, to take the time to allow joy to happen in us.

Son, I honor your compassion. I see you bringing joy into the lives of people around you by serving their needs. I invite you to use some of your strength and some of your love to identify and to satisfy your own needs. You, too, are worth it. You, too, are worthy of joy.

The "Be A Man" Box

My wife gets her seventh-grade kids involved in this wonderful event called "Challenge Day." Challenge Day is all about opening these budding adolescents to their feelings—all the stuff they've felt compelled to stuff inside.

One of those stuffing spots is the "Be A Man" Box. This box teaches boys exactly what they're supposed to do to be Men:

Shut up!

Suck it up!

These are the marching orders they have been given instead of The Blessing.

Shut up! You're not loving; you're not supposed to be loving; you're a wimp if you talk about what you're feeling. Sadness, fear, shame, and even anger are not welcome here. What are you, a crybaby?

Suck it up! You're not inherently powerful; you're only powerful if you gut it out and never say a word about how alone you feel, how scared you feel. How small you feel. What are you, a wimp?

And, in the absence of The Blessing, in the absence of father-men who can give The Blessing, this is exactly what most boys do:

Shut up!

Suck it up!

This is what their fathers tell them to do. This is what their stepfathers tell them to do. This is what their teachers tell them to do. This is what their coaches tell them to do. This is what the drill sergeant tells them to do.

Shut up!

Suck it up!

And most do as they're told, as they've seen modeled. They are so hungry for father-love, they do it...

Until they explode—or implode. Until they spew out all that sadness, fear, shame, and anger on the world—on women, rivals, the environment. Or on themselves in the form of addictions, depression, suicide.

Son, can I tell you what I think a man is supposed to do? A man speaks up—speaks his feelings, speaks his truth. A man stands up for the needs of others and himself. A man is too strong, too loving to live in any "Shut up! Suck it up!" box. And you, you have all you need to be such a strong, loving man.

"*I am not worthy!*"

Wayne and Garth of "Wayne's World" on their knees,
> bowing—"I am not worthy!"
> bowing—"I am not worthy!"
> bowing—"I am not worthy!"

They always cracked me up with that bit—Wayne and Garth, the ultimate boys, spaced out in their basement, no father or mother in sight, doing the best they could, making it up as they went along, bowing and chanting with all their loser innocence to Aerosmith or Christie Brinkley.

When I've seen other boys bow down to big-chested athletes or long-legged actresses—"I am not worthy! I am not worthy!"—I've been less amused. Not only because it was copycat, but also because I sensed the truth beneath their words.

"I am not worthy!"

I've had a voice in me shouting that 24/7 for longer than I care to remember. Not that I hear it most of the time. I'd die if I heard it most of the time. I've built up all kinds of defenses and offenses not to hear it. Rescuing others; obsessing on details; reading self-help books; ignoring my emotions—all of these lower the volume of this voice. Temporarily.

"I am not worthy!"

This is my shame talking. And as far as I can tell, for most men, shame is the deepest, the darkest of our emotions. We might feel uncomfortable with, or even appalled by our sadness, our anger, and our fear; but we will do almost anything to avoid shame. In fact, the way I look at it, these other emotions are layered above our deep, primary shame. So if we even get a whiff of it, we may well get angry—or sad—or fearful—as a way to protect us, or distract us, from our shame.

Our primary shame is our unshakable feeling of not being man enough, of being weak and unlovable. Of our fundamental un-worthiness.

The antidote for this seemingly bottomless worthlessness is The Blessing.

Son, I am sad you feel unworthy. I feel the pain of your shame, and I see you struggling to protect yourself from it. Let me bow down to you now, three times, and tell you this from the bottom of my heart: You are a strong, loving man worthy of love. You are a strong, loving man worthy of love. You are a strong, loving man worthy of love.

"It's not your fault"

I love movies where guys are tight—kid each other, pick with each other, even fight with each other—but in the end, are loyal to each other. Love each other. I love movies that revolve around lost sons—sons full of anger, fear, sadness, and shame. I love movies that make me laugh my ass off one minute, and cry the next. I love movies with underdogs; I love movies that have working-class heroes. I love movies set in Boston. I love movies starring Matt Damon.

Which are some of the reasons why I love *Good Will Hunting*.

In his book *Wild at Heart*, John Eldredge quotes a pivotal chunk near the end of that movie. It's the scene where Robin Williams, playing a tough but bighearted therapist named Sean, finally has a break through with Damon's character, Will Hunting, a twenty-one year-old emotionally shut-down genius from the wrong side of the tracks. That Will had been mercilessly and repeatedly beaten by his drunken foster father is all documented in the file in Sean's hands.

Sean:	*Hey, Will…I don't know a lot, but you see this (holding his file)…This is not your fault.*
Will:	*Yeah, I know that.*
Sean:	*Look at me, son. It's not your fault.*
Will:	*I know.*
Sean:	*It's not your fault.*
Will:	*(Beginning to grow defensive) I know.*
Sean:	*No, no, you don't. It's not your fault.*
Will:	*(Really defensive) I know.*
Sean:	*It's not your fault.*
Will:	*(Trying to end the conversation) All right.*
Sean:	*It's not your fault…it's not your fault.*

Will:	*(Anger) Don't fuck with me, Sean, not you.*
Sean:	*It's not your fault…it's not your fault…it's not your fault.*
Will:	*(Collapses into his arms, weeping) I'm so sorry; I'm so sorry.*

At this point, the stage directions in the screenplay read, *"Two lonely souls being father and son together."*

Exactly. Two lonely souls being father and son together.

And in words that sound to me like Blessing, both of the father and the son, Eldredge writes: *"It is no shame that you need healing; it is no shame to look to another for strength; it is no shame that you feel young and afraid inside. It's not your fault."*

BLESSING OUR BODY

My Father Had a 4-Foot Penis

When I was young
   my father had a four-foot penis

When I turned my head
   he watered the front lawn with it
   he steered the car with it
   he teed-off with it
   he beat our behinds with it

It was the length and dark color of the shotguns
   mounted on the den room wall
It was heftier than the thick logs
he heaped on the Christmas fire

It was a lightning rod
It was a water tower
It was Moses's staff and Tarzan's spear
It was John Henry's hammer and
   Hank Aaron's bat

It lay coiled in his pants like a rattlesnake
   curled up like gym rope
   wound tight like black tire
   twisted like Watergate tapes

We never saw it, my brother and I
(he kept it behind closed doors)
but we dreamed big, bad dreams

And I built my life around this four-foot fact:
the come-up-short son bent on Nice
the second-stringer too scared to star

When I was middle-aged
    and my father was dying
I was dying to lift
his hospital sheets and peek:
to once and for all
measure my manhood

But I couldn't
I was afraid I'd find
not the prized cock of my childhood
    but a poor limp wounded worm
      no longer than my little finger

Not much victory there
just more guilt, sadness, anger
    and fear—
Then what?

How to live once Oz has shriveled?
How to grow once God has shrunk?

I am writing long poems
    about fathers and sons
      (about Peter's peter)
until my own son comes along

I will show him my penis
I will tell him not to worry
    his own tiny snail & peas
      will grow into a handsome cock & balls
I will tell him how I once thought my father's penis
    was the size of a Giant's Crayola crayon

I will tell him, One day
*   you will walk through this world*
feeling the power of a god
*   with a four-foot penis*
and the love of a god
*   with an eight-chambered heart*

Men's Bodies

Our bodies don't seem to belong to us. They are lost continents, Africas, divorced from us. Out there somewhere most of the time while we're up here, in our heads.

Our bodies are biceps, pecs, calves—and not much else.

Our bodies hurt, so we ignore the hurt. No pain, no gain. Work it out, work through it.

I've always felt inadequate in relation to other men's bodies, black men's bodies…my father's body.

My father never said very much about his body. There were whispers of an ulcer soon after he started his own business. An occasional headache. Little else. His body seemed indestructible. His back was absolutely whale-like. His pulse a spectacularly low 50–55 beats per minute.

He would live to be 100.

He died at 63.

His body had been telling him for decades he was riddled with fear and sadness and shame, but my father couldn't hear it, or he ignored it.

I've sat in the middle of a circle of men and asked them to place their hands on my head, my shoulders, my stomach, and my back while they told me what they honored in me. Eyes closed, I felt the warmth of their hands and their words draw the sadness and the pain and the fear out of me. I've done this three times. I've cried tears of joy each time.

The Blessing involves bodies. A father's, a son's. A hug, two strong hands on the shoulders, eye-to-eye. Intimate connection. I think some of the father's strength is pressed into a son when he hugs him, looks in his eyes, Blesses him. It's a beacon that finds its way to his son's seed, turns it on, lights it up.

Son, your body is OK just the way it is. It's not too small, it's not too big; it's perfect. It is just what it should be. And your body is wise. Listen to it, listen to its wisdom. Let it lead you out of your head and into your heart—into your feelings. Your body is made of strength and love, and your body is built for strength and love. How can you be anything but a strong, loving man?

No Pain, No Gain

I've heard a thousand guys—and very few women—say it: "No pain, No gain." I've said it myself. Hell, I've *lived* it. I watched my Dad live it.

I remember my Dad telling me that if you only did ten push-ups every night, even if you did them every night for the rest of your life, you wouldn't get any stronger. In other words: Boy, if you want to get stronger—and what boy doesn't!—you need to do *11* tonight, 12 tomorrow, 13 on Wednesday….

Got it: No pain, No Gain.

And, as with most clichés, there's some truth here. In one sense, a great deal of truth, perhaps. Pain is absolutely part of what it means to be human, and how we deal with pain is crucial to our growth. Although "Slacker" is at least partly in these days, much of America still believes you should be disciplined enough to reach a certain level of pain—and then push through it and do one more…One more push-up, one more rep, one more phone call, even one more minute on the meditation cushion…Your reward, your pay-off, your growth, your strength—is on the other side of that pain.

Fine. But I contend there is something fucked-up here, as well. Particularly when it comes to men.

Most men I know, including myself, don't believe we're strong enough, neither physically nor emotionally. We need to get stronger, or at least, look stronger. We're not enough, not man enough, as we are. That is what my father was unconsciously telling me. And "No pain, no gain" is the formula we erroneously believe will transform us into Men: Come on, one more push-up, Petey!

For years, part of me has wanted to lift weights until my pecs popped and my biceps danced. I had moments where I wanted to side step all my stunted psychological growth, and just grab some barbells and **GET BIG**. Maybe I've been too hard on myself here; maybe I could get bigger physically and it wouldn't be a side step or a cover-up. I'm certainly not suggesting that men shouldn't exercise and feel good about their bodies.

But I do think we "No pain, no gain," gym-bound guys are harboring a secret illusion: We men want to believe that if we get *physically* stronger, we will be *emotionally* stronger too; it's a package deal, we hope. And sometimes, it is: a man gets physically fit and feels more emotionally fit, as well. But much of the time, more muscle is just a cover-up; more muscle is just more armor; more muscle is just the appearance of strength—the Little Boy inside is still just as scared.

The Blessing reminds a man of his inherent strength and soothes the Little Boy.

Son, you have all the strength you need to be a strong man right inside of you, right now. Do push-ups, lift weights, do what you need to do to feel the strength of your body—and do what you need to do to feel the strength of your heart: join a men's group, get therapy, write poems, pray.... But please never forget that you have everything you need inside you to be a powerful, loving man. You are enough, now.

Back Pain

What man hasn't had back pain?

I certainly have. Hospitalized at 16—two weeks of traction, one girdle-to-go. A visit the following year to the New York Giant's orthopedic surgeon: "Juvenile disc," he called it. "Let's operate." I was 17; my dad and I looked at him like he was crazy. Out to Pasadena where I spent nine days with Dr. Leroy Perry, a famous sports chiropractor. "Lose the girdle," Perry said," or you *will* have to have an operation." Then a regime of stretching, heat, ice, stretching, heat, ice. That helped; I was physically more flexible. After Dr. Perry, innumerable preventative trips to the chiropractor; a streak of close to ten years of nightly back exercises.... And still, inevitably, at least once a year—usually somewhere between Christmas and New Year's—I would endure a terrible week of pain where, wracked with spasms, I crawled on-all-fours around the house, literally unable to stand up. For years on end this painful pattern persisted.

Until, at 32, a colleague handed me Dr. John Sarno's *Healing Back Pain: The Mind-Body Connection.*

Sarno's premise: 98% of the back cases he sees as a doctor of orthopedic medicine have nothing to do with disc problems, or pinched nerves, or physical trauma; rather, the back pain is a manifestation of unexamined, unacknowledged anger and anxiety. More precisely, our back pain is a defense mechanism against repressed emotional pain: we become fixated on the physical pain and what we believe are its physical causes, and therefore avoid having to deal with the underlying anger and anxiety.

His recommended treatment: *Think psychological, not physical.*

> I suggest to patients that when they find them-selves being aware of the pain they must consciously and forcefully shift their attention to something psychological, like something they are worried about, a chronic family or financial problem, a recurrent source of irritation, any-thing in the psychological realm, for that sends a message to the brain that they're no longer deceived by the pain. When that message reaches the depths of the mind, the subconscious, the pain ceases. (77)

Was I skeptical? Damn right I was! Part of me held tight to the idea that my pain was caused by a *physical* event—that fall I took sophomore year, my "narrow spinal column," my slight scoliosis—and that it could only be corrected by *physical* means: back exercises, correct posture, chiropractic adjustments, heel lifts. And I was even willing to concede, given the post-semester/Christmas pattern of severe lower back spasms, that my back pain had something to do with "stress." But to fully accept the idea that the cause of my physical pain was, ultimately, *emotional* pain—from repressed anger, fear, anxiety? Ouch!!

But, gingerly, I tried it. When I felt a twitch of spasm, I asked myself, "Ok, what am I angry about, or sad about, or fearful about?" Sometimes I got immediate relief; sometimes I had to persist, to stay focused on my emotions, before the pain eased; sometimes, no matter how much I zeroed in on my anger or anxiety, the pain won.

I can report this, however: in the thirteen years since reading (and re-reading) Sarno's book, I've had only one incident of lower back spasms. And to be honest, even that one time was comparatively mild—spasms, yes, but not severe enough to reduce me to baby crawl. Do I still have back pain? Yep. Mostly mild shoulder and neck stuff—and I've found, as Sarno predicts, that this too is directly linked to whatever emotions I'm currently out-of-touch with.

We men will endure almost anything to avoid dealing with our anger and anxiety. Even severe back pain.

Son, it hurts me to see you in such pain. I know you believe your pain comes from lifting or twisting this or playing that. And maybe it does. Could you also consider that the pain might be tied to your emotions? Could you ask yourself what you're angry about in your life, what you're sad about, what you're fearful of? Could you begin to see your pain as a helpful indicator of something in your emotional life that needs some attention? Could you come to believe that your body is strong, that your body knows, that your body is your friend?

Boy in a Rowboat

There's a painting hanging in our guest room of a boy in a rowboat. The boy, maybe thirteen or fourteen, is shirtless; the lightly tinted muscles of his shoulders and back hint of the powerful man he will one day be. He is looking down and off to the side, maybe at ripples on the invisible water, maybe at his own reflection. I can tell he can feel the sun heating his back, can smell the sweat under his arms and running down his sides to his cut-offs. He is bowed slightly forward, coasting, waiting to dip the oar heads back in the water again, gathering himself for the next stroke when he will pull hard with his shoulders and biceps and back and push hard with his legs. Waiting for that moment when, feeling the boat suddenly shoot ahead, he will once again feel his own power.

I have been that boy in that rowboat. In the early Seventies, I rowed myself around and around little Galway Lake. I loved the smell of the sun on the old gray wood and the nearly silent seam the boat cut in the lake. I loved to dip, and drift, dip and drift, dip…and drift. And I also loved to pull those oars with all my might through the thick water—again, and again, and again, and again, and again—until the boat was racing along.

Rowing was meditation, masturbation, celebration.

Here in this boat, out in the middle of a lake on a June afternoon was one of the few places in my teenage world where I felt alone but not lonely; peaceful, not pressed. Here in this boat was where I was most aware of my adolescent body—of my sweat, my swollen muscles, my potential strength. Here in this boat was the one and only place in my boy's life where I felt powerful.

If a lake could talk, this might be The Blessing it would give to boys in rowboats:

Son, I celebrate your solitude and your strength. May you find peace in my lap, and may you ride on my shoulders all the way to manhood.

Is There Life After Basketball?

I have this movie idea: A thirty-nine-year-old suburban sports psychologist has a radio talk show called "Dr. Hoop." Aging (ex-) athletes call up so the good Doctor (his actual name is Marvin) can help ease their retirement from whatever sport they have been playing all their lives. Of course, Marvin, a long-time hooper himself, not to mention a social activist, thinks he has it all under control; he could give up his own inner city pick-up basketball anytime he wanted to. His wife wants him to (it's "dangerous"); his six-year-old son wants him to (he likes catching butterflies). But Marvin doesn't want to, and he somehow believes his sports-drunk father doesn't want him to, either. His Achilles heel is his Achilles heel—he tears it ten minutes into the movie—and his whole life gets torn up as well.

The tag line on the movie poster: **"Is There Life After Basketball?"**

That's not an easy question for a lot of men to answer. For many of us, myself included, sports has been the one direct connection to our fathers. Often our only connection, and our primary language.

Like Marvin, we've tossed a baseball back and forth with our fathers in peaceful summer silence, walked dreamy green fairways side-by-side on summer evenings. Together, we've watched Super Bowls and super dunks and superstars in every sport. Our fathers have watched us dribble up and down a thousand courts, toss balls of all shapes through a thousand springs and a thousand falls, cheered as we swam and skated and ran…. Or they never showed up for any of our games, and we did it anyway, hoping one day they would.

And let me tell you, we played our asses off. For him, for our father. Present or absent, in the stands cheering or out of our lives drinking, more than teammates, more than girls, *he* was the one we were trying to win over. Our father. We believed that if we scored enough goals or points, if we won enough games or races, if we made enough jump shots or putts, our father would slip The Blessing over our neck like a gold medal.

So what do you mean it's time to stop playing basketball?!

If basketball is my best shot at winning my father's Blessing, and I'm still desperate to win that Blessing and become a man, how the hell can I quit?! You might as well ask me to cut off my penis.

Cut to "Dr Hoop." The last scene of the movie. Marvin's in the studio on the phone line talking to some Triathlon champ who has lost a leg in a motorcycle accident or some high school fastball phenom whose arm gave out or some ex-college running back who just blew out his ACL playing Saturday football with his buddies. Or some radio-talk show host who recently ripped his Achilles playing pick-up on the west side of Detroit. He's saying:

Fellow Jocks, you're feeling like a part of your life is over. A big part of your life, something that has defined your manhood for decades. Without my sport, I'm nothing—that's what we think. Without my sport, I'm weak. A failure. A boy with no possibility of winning my father's love—and becoming a man. I'm here to tell you that you could run for more yards than Barry, win more rings than Michael, make more putts than Tiger—and you will still come up short. Still feel weak. Still fail to win your father's love. Still feel like a lost boy in a world of men.

I'm also here to tell you that before *you scored your first touchdown or won your first race—before you even* thought *of scoring or running—you already had inside of you all it takes to be a strong, loving man. You were born with seeds of strength and love, just as surely as you were born with biceps and lungs. That your father didn't tell you that each night before you went to bed, that your coaches didn't tell you that at least once in their half-time talks, is a tragedy. But I'm telling you now: even if you never throw another strike or dunk another basketball—or, like me, have* never dunked *a basketball—you are a strong, loving man.*

And fellow Jocks, I invite you to spread this Blessing, pass it on to other young boys who are throwing balls and slapping pucks. Pass it on to your sons. As you teach them the fundamentals of their sport, teach them this fundamental truth: even if they never win a trophy or score a point, they have all it takes to be strong, loving men.

Hugs

It's sad to me, the way men hug.

Most man-to-man hugs look like this: put one foot forward, lean in real quick, "Pat-Pat-Pat" on the back—and separate. Awkwardly.

Then there's the Hip-Hop Hug: out of a handshake, pull each other into a quick little shoulder-hug. Though it looks much cooler than "Pat-Pat-Pat," it's a half-a-hug at best.

For special occasions, there is the Victory hug: this is a kind of a dance step with the two men more committed to yelling some variation of "We won!" than they are to hugging.

For most occasions, shaking hands is just fine, thank you.

I've grown to like hugging men.

We hug each other every Monday night in my men's group. John has got the best bear hug in the business. He throws his arms around you, pulls you in, and holds you there for maybe a five-count. I feel his strength, his love when he hugs me like that. John has a couple of sons. He hugs them the same way.

I would have given anything for a hug like that from my father.

I can't remember ever getting any kind of hug from him, and I can't remember him ever hugging another man. Not even Howard, his best friend of thirty years—a big guy who I imagine could, in the right circumstances, give one helluva bear hug himself.

Most men are afraid to hug. Most men are afraid to do anything physical with each other that doesn't fall under the safe category of "Sports."

For most men, hugging, even the mere thought of hugging, triggers our homophobia. Hugging men means I'm gay, might mean I'm gay, may be perceived as my being gay. But a man hugging another man is not, automatically, a sexual act; it can be an intimate communication—and there's a difference.

A hug can communicate The Blessing. Finally, no words are even needed. Here's what a loving, authentic hug says to a son, a boy, a man:

You exist. You matter to me. I'm not afraid of your strength or your love or your body, and you need not be afraid of mine. Straight or gay, we are two strong, loving men.

The Catcher in the Rye

The Catcher in the Rye is my all-time favorite novel. And Holden Caulfield gets my vote for the funniest, most sensitive, most truth-telling Unblessed boy in all of literature.

Holden is sixteen going on sixty, and his life is falling apart. He's been kicked out of school. Again. Everywhere he turns, phonies are climbing in through the goddamn window; and his classmate, James Castle, has jumped out the window to his death. Holden's father thinks military school, not The Blessing, is the answer.

So with nowhere to go, Holden shows up at Mr. Antolini's apartment. Antolini is Holden's old English teacher and a family friend; he was also the only one willing to pick up James Castle after he jumped. He immediately recognizes Holden is heading for a fall of his own and gives him some sound advice: "'The mark of an immature man is that he wants to die nobly for a cause, while the mark of the mature man is that he wants to live humbly for one.'" Exhausted, and feeling safe, Holden falls asleep.

He wakes up to find Mr. Antolini gently patting him on the head. Holden freaks. Suddenly Antolini's a "flit," and Holden, hinting at past abuse, flees.

In Holden's world, when a man touches you, he can only be "perverty." In Holden's world, it's inconceivable that a father could bestow The Blessing on his son. That's why Holden wants to be the Catcher in the Rye: When all the little kids, all the Unblessed little kids, are about to fall off this crazy cliff…he'd be there to catch them.

Holden instinctively knows what Antolini knows: it's only a matter of time before an Unblessed boy takes a serious fall. And if you want to know the truth, maybe Antolini was only trying to give Holden the one thing, The Blessing, that might prevent that fall.

Holden, I'm sorry I scared you. I'm sorry you thought there was anything sexual about my touching your head. And I'm deeply, deeply sorry if anybody in the past has done anything sexually to you without your consent; if so, they were horribly wrong, and it wasn't your fault. I only wanted to tell you what a wonderful young man you are:

smart and funny and sensitive. And although you may doubt it now, you have all you need to be a mature man, a strong, loving man—a Blesser in the Rye.

Sexual Abuse

I know a number of men who were sexually abused when they were young. By neighbors, by uncles, by their fathers.

I can only imagine what that does to a boy.

A boy craves The Blessing. He is looking for the men in his life to see the future man in himself—to honor his inherent power and love.

Instead, when sexually abused, that boy learns he is powerless and that love, at least with respect to him, is perverse. Men, whose role it is to nurture a boy's strength and to model love, have inflicted the ultimate non-Blessing, delivered the deepest Curse. Maybe the worst thing that happens to such a boy is that he loses his trust of men: understandably cutting himself off from the community of men, he is left alone in the wilderness of his own shame and pain.

Some boys never recover from this. Some boys feel powerless and unlovable—and alone—for the rest of their lives.

And yet I know some sexually abused men who have taken on the mission of healing themselves. They seek to recover what was stolen from them by their abusers: their capacity to use their power to set boundaries and to give and receive love.

And to trust men again. The men I know understand that though it was a man who hurt them, it can only be men who will heal them. They have found the miraculous courage to show other men their deepest wounds, to expose their anger and their sadness and their fear and their shame. And in so doing, they have not only touched joy themselves, but have brought joy to me and other men who have witnessed their powerful work.

Brother, I feel your incredible pain and I honor your beautiful courage. You have made me painstakingly aware of my right and my power to set boundaries, and you have shown me how to open up the deepest, most shame-filled parts of myself for healing. Thanks to your courage, I experienced the loving power of men. I bless you on your healing journey.

Son, what I did to you is unforgivable. I won't even ask your forgiveness. Let me only say what I was too weak, too confused to say years ago: you have all you need to be a strong, loving man. Nobody, nobody can take that from you. You have proven that, and I'm proud of you.

Penis Size

When I was nearly 40, a woman I was dating told me I had a big penis.

"Really?" I was incredulous. Pleased, oh my god yes, but incredulous.

For a couple of days, I actually believed it. I walked differently in the world, my penis suddenly banging against the inside of my jockey shorts. I was no longer a tiptoeing boy; I was a man with a big dick—so watch the **fuck** out!

But then I remembered hearing that any smart woman would tell her man he had a big penis. Women know men are hugely insecure on this score, and it only made sense to reassure your lover he had one awesome cock.

I went back to her with this, and she held her ground. She gave me some data to back up her claim. Men like data, but data on this all-important topic didn't mean squat.

What good was data when I looked down after a shower at a diminutive, timid mushroom? The mirror did not lie: I had no hang.

The joy in my jockey shorts diminished. My manpower drooped. At the very best, when supremely erect, and for no longer than half-an-hour, I had a statistically slightly above-average penis. Most of the time, when it came to penis size—when it came to feeling my power as a man—I was a boy again.

I never saw my father's penis. But given his bulk and his deep voice, the way he commanded his house and throned himself in his leather chair, the way the outside world treated him with utter respect even before he pulled out his thick roll of clean hundred-dollar bills, I knew he possessed a King's cock, a magnificent four-footer, a rattlesnake to my inch-worm.

And to this day, as silly as I know that is, part of me still believes it. His rattlesnake to my inchworm. He is long dead and buried, but his enormous, res-erected penis lives on.

In this Unblessed world, penis-size = Power.

No wonder boys and men are always wondering, Am I big enough? We're always quietly asking ourselves that question because most of the time we don't feel big at all. We felt small next to our fathers, and we still feel small. Our tiny peckers are only a metaphor for our overall smallness, our overall sense of powerlessness. And no woman, however honest and well intentioned, can convince us otherwise.

But we men can talk about our penises, share our fears, speak to our shame and our powerlessness. We can share the dirty little secret we all harbor: I have the tiniest dick on the planet. ("No, *I* do!") We can bless our cocks, and move on.

The Blessing bestows bigness.

Son, you are big enough. Don't worry, your muscles will grow, your mind will grow. Your heart will grow. And yes, your beautiful cock and balls will grow too. Though it may not feel like it to you, though you may look in the mirror and doubt it, I am telling you the truth: you have all the ingredients inside of you, right now, to grow into a beautiful, strong, and loving man.

Boxing Gloves

My wife and I got my nephew two pairs of boxing gloves for Christmas this year. Bright red 9 oz. Everlasts. Perfect for him and his buddy to beat up on each other some. At least that was the idea.

Christmas morning, though, father and son went at it first in the family room/boxing ring.

In this corner, at 40 years-old and weighing 160 lbs, the father and reigning Champion of the House, Billy "Go Irish!" McPartlon; and in this corner, 12 years-old and weighing 85 lbs, the son and perennial challenger, William "The Ostrich" McPartlon.

A jab from the challenger—deflection. Jab, jab—deflections. "Kidney punch! Kidney punch!" yells Billy, though it's hard to tell whether he's giving them or getting them. Tied up now. Break. More boyish jabs and infectious laughter. Ohhs and ahhs and huff puffing. And then, deep in Round 3, the challenger unleashes a score to the side of the champ's head! A series of right and left hooks from the son! Father Billy seems to be in trouble. No, no, sports fans, he's still laughing, waiting, ropa-doping…And now counter-attacking his raucously thrilled son.

I've always loved the way William and Billy roughhouse with each other—tickle-fests, all-star wrestling, bumping and grabbing. This fall, they played Sunday lacrosse together. A little boxing was inevitable.

I have fought my own father in dreams, in poems. He was a boxer in the service, a good one. 26-2. He had a cut line over his left eye that he said he got in one of those two losses. Had we fought for real, it would have been no contest.

I didn't want to fight him. At least not when I was young. But I did want to roughhouse with him like Billy does with William. I wanted to wrestle with him on the family room floor; I wanted to jump on his back; I wanted him to grab my foot and my hand and fly me like a jet plane out on the front lawn, landing me with a soft bump on the summer-smelling grass.

If he had done that, maybe I wouldn't have wanted to fight him in my later years, after he had died. Maybe my brother wouldn't have had to square off to fight him in that same family room when he was 18 and I was away at college.

Roughhousing, wrestling, boxing…it's all part of The Blessing.

Son, you have all you need to be Champion of the House. You have strong arms and a strong heart. Let's slip on some gloves and go a couple of rounds, give each other our best shot. And at the end, like Rocky and Apollo, let's hug each other and raise each other's hands over our heads in victory.

BLESSING THE GOOD BOY, THE BAD BOY, AND EVERY BOY IN BETWEEN

Dylan

1974 or 1975. I ask my dad if we can watch the Bob Dylan concert on TV.
"Who's Bob Dylan?" he wants to know.
Then he sees for himself. Dylan singing "Tangled Up in Blue." My father loves Nat King Cole; Dylan doesn't sound anything like Nat King Cole. And his feather earring, eye shadow, and fur coat don't help things.
"Change the channel," he says.
That hurt. At that point I really didn't know all that much about Bob Dylan myself. But I knew he represented something new and strange and important. He was only seven years younger than my father, but his was a different world—the world I was entering. A post-60s, post-Watergate world. A poet's world, an artist's world. A world larger than crew cuts, business, and Schenectady, NY.
From my father's perspective, Dylan's was a scary world. A world that could gobble up a Good Boy like me fast as Jack Flash. I understand that better now.
Still, when I was fifteen, sixteen, I wanted my father to understand something important about me. I was more than the clean-cut kid who always brought home straight "A"s and stayed out of trouble. I wanted him to see the rebel in me. To honor that rebel. I wanted to feel like I could look like Bob Dylan and write poetry like Bob Dylan and sing like Bob Dylan—and he would still love me. Maybe love me even more because I was bold enough to be so bold. So creative.
Impossible, I know. But that's what I wanted. Twenty years earlier, I bet Dylan had wanted the same thing from his father.
I get up slowly and walk to the big Zenith in our family room. Dylan is just slipping into "Lay Lady, Lay." I click the dial to something safer—"Gunsmoke," maybe. I walk back and sit down on the couch without looking at my father in his leather chair. In my head I'm singing

Lay Lady, lay. Lay across my big brass bed.

The Good Boy

I wrote the book on The Good Boy.

I got straight "A"s from kindergarten through senior year. "Please" and "Thank you" were as automatic as flushing the toilet. I answered the phone, "Hello, this is Peter, can I help you please?" Every time. On the basketball team from eighth grade on, president of my class three years in a row. No real drinking, no drugs, no sex…I was such a Good Boy it was disgusting.

Why? Why would any boy choose such a straightforward, no-nonsense, boring road?

Two simple reasons: (1) I was afraid of my father, so it was just a smart survival choice to do exactly what I was supposed to do and not piss him off. (2) I thought being the ultimate Good Boy would earn me The Blessing.

I was wrong about The Blessing part.

OK. My father didn't kill me. But just because he rarely exploded at me like he did at my Bad Boy brother doesn't mean I got The Blessing. You can get trapped being a Good Boy; I got trapped being a Good Boy. Once a Good Boy, always a Good Boy. Encore after encore of Goodness, all in the hope that this "A," this award, this athletic accomplishment will earn The Blessing.

I had it backwards.

Being the world's goodiest Good Boy was never going to get me The Blessing; I was a fanatical Good Boy because I *never got* The Blessing. I became a Good Boy out of the fear of "I'm not Good," "I'm not Enough"—therefore, "I need to *prove* I'm Good."

The Blessing has nothing to do with fear and performance. The Blessing is all about love and basic goodness.

Son, you were good on the day you were born, and you will be good on the day you die. You have within you a basic goodness. You may forget that somewhere down the road, you may believe that being good is all about doing good, proving you're good. Performing. I invite you then to relax, and to trust, instead, in your inherent goodness. And when you do, only good will follow.

The Bad Boy

Since I had already signed up for the part of The Good Boy, my brother got stuck with playing The Bad Boy.

He slingshot rocks at cars. He talked back to my mother and eased his way to "B"s and "C"s. He got more than his share of "you've-been-bad" beatings. Which didn't stop him from sneaking out his window at night like Huck Finn. Or pushing my father's car out of the garage and racing it on the backroads at 100 mph. He smoked pot, sold it; had sex, liked it.

I was the front-row pleaser; Paul was the back-row weasel. I hid my anger—he stoked it, smoked it. We were both, each in our own way, begging for The Blessing.

Bad Boys are everywhere. Hanging out, smoking, fighting, killing themselves, each other, time…waiting for their fathers to show up.

And when the father does show up, he usually shows up Cursing: You're no good, you're a fuck-up, a loser, always have been, always will be—maybe this will fix you! And then the Cursing turns into a beating, or if the Bad Boy is old enough, a brawl.

Yes, the Bad Boys are waiting for their fathers to show up…not to Curse them, but to Bless them. They might pretend that's not true, not cool, Fuck you!—but that's all they want. All they've ever wanted.

Son, I see you're angry, and your anger is welcome here. I'm sorry if I used my strength to hurt you, if my own anger and fear and pain got in the way of my love. Let me tell you now what I meant to tell you then, when you were born, and every day after: You're not Bad; you're not a Bad Boy. You are a beautiful, strong, loving man. And I don't want to fight you, I want to hug you. May I hug you?

The Eternal Boy

Puer Aeternus, the eternal boy. The boy who refuses to grow up. The boy who stays up in his head, likes high, abstract places. Likes to fly, stay dry. The Little Prince, Peter Pan, Peter Parker…Peter Putnam.

Guilty as charged. It was safer up in my head. Ideals could live up there, uncorrupted by day-to-day dirt. Safer up in my bedroom with my books—downstairs, my dad in his chair, TV blaring nonsense.

I vowed to stay up there as long as I could.

"When are you going to get married?"

"No time soon."

"Kids?"

"I'm a kid! Kids scare me."

What will bring a high-flying boy down to earth?

Maybe when he gets sick and tired of the same relationships: he's always up here, she's always down there. Maybe when his father dies, and he has a dream.

> I'm in a small airplane with my father. He's sleeping. There's a voice coming in over the radio, one of his friends, calling for him. Dad doesn't wake up. I finally pick it up. The voice tells me to try to awaken him, so I do. He's really, deeply asleep. I shake him. His face is way back under a bed in the plane. I finally tell him we're coming in for a landing. He does wake up, sits up for a second. I can see his round, steroid-puffy face as he says, "We're OK." He lies back down. I'm afraid he's going to fall back asleep and I'm going to have to land the plane myself somehow.

Two months after the dream, the eternal boy goes to a New Warrior Weekend. There are other boys there, many of them way up in their heads, scared to death, afraid of crashing. Just like him. After the Weekend, for months, in the presence of other men, he begins owning all that fear, all that anger, all that sadness, all that shame—slowly lowering himself down into his emotions, into his body.

One day, he finally believes what his father said to him in the dream. "We're OK." The plane is safely landed, Peter Pan is grounded. He swings open the door and walks out a man.

Mama's Boy

I know some full-fledged Mama's Boys. For good reason, they have completely rejected their fathers. Their fathers were abusers, batterers, drinkers, abandoners. These boys then completely embraced their mothers. They became their mother's ultimate Good Son, their confidante, or even a surrogate husband. They would never, never do what they had seen their fathers do to their mother. They made a pact, perhaps consciously, certainly unconsciously, to treat their mothers like queens, and most importantly, to never, ever leave their mothers.

And who could blame them? A boy needs to survive, a boy needs love. If the father is a threat to his survival or is nowhere in sight; if a father is seemingly attempting to kill or to abandon a boy's other pillar of survival and love, his mother, the most "natural" thing in the world is for this boy to pledge eternal allegiance to his mother.

But then that boy grows up.

Or tries to. But an essential part of a boy's growing up, of his becoming a man, is finding the means to break from mother energy and step into the energy of father—into the community of men and manhood.

For a Mama's boy—and for his mother—such a step feels like the ultimate betrayal. Like murder. Actually, that's true for any boy and his mother—just more true, more painful, for a boy who has had to make this necessary yet twisted pact.

And yet, soon enough, there's something else kicking in: resentment. Probably it's been there for a long time, this boy's anger at his mother. Maybe he's been able to stuff most of it and keep up the Good Son; maybe it's leaked out some—angry words, rebellious gestures. But it's on the rise, this nasty resentment, and a son can do what he can to stuff it back into shadow. But it will not be denied or repressed or ignored forever. In fact, the longer he goes without breaking from mother energy, the more he feels trapped by this energy. There's something in a man that will not rest until there is healthiness and wholeness, and at a certain point, this Mama-bond isn't healthy.

I can speak to this because I have experienced it, to some extent, with my mother. And I have witnessed it and analyzed it with one of my best friends. I have also seen it manifested in several black men I know personally, and it appears to me to be a prevalent dynamic in the frequently fatherless African-American community.

So what's a Mama's boy to do?

He has an incredibly difficult choice to make: continue stuffing and remain a Mama's boy…or break the bond and step into his manhood.

If he chooses the latter, he will need a "father," an Elder, or a circle of men—some strong, loving masculine force to help him break the feminine force bonding him to boyhood. What's needed is an immersion in masculinity, a Baptism, an initiation into the Land of the Fathers.

It's important to say that this does not mean the end of his relationship with his mother; it does mean, however, that the relationship will change in some fundamental way. Ideally, the son-mother dynamic, which had been unnaturally sustained and increasingly strained, would be more authentic: more like two adults with clear boundaries who are able to cleanly speak their wants and needs to each other.

Three Blessings to end with: one from a father; one from a strong, loving man; one from a mother.

Son, I honor the way you stepped in to take care of your mother. That was my responsibility, and I am deeply sorry for not meeting it. I am sorry for the pain it caused you and your mother. I see you now stepping into your power—into your manhood. I admire your strength and your continued love.

Brother, I see how painful this is, and I honor your courage. You took care of business in the only way you could—by taking care of your mother—and now you are doing what is necessary to take care of yourself. I have great respect for the difficult, new boundaries you are drawing. I see what a powerful, loving man you are, and I will be here for you as you continue with your healing work.

Son, thank you for all you gave to me. You were a beautiful boy, and now it is time for you to become a beautiful man. Please understand that I'm OK. I am doing what I need to do to feel strong and whole—and I want you to do the same. Find the men you need to help support you be the man you are. Like millions of mothers for thousands of years, I will be here when you return, and then we will talk, one strong, loving woman to one powerful, loving man.

The Man of the House

Somebody needs to be the man of the house. A house is not a home without a man. A boy can't be Blessed without a man around.

My friend's father left when he was ten. His devastated older brother hid in his room. By default, he became the man of the house.

So when his mother washed the dishes every night, my friend sat at the kitchen table and listened to her. He listened to her sadness, felt her anger, tried his desperate best to solve her problems. He was no longer her ten-year-old son; he was her peer, her friend, her surrogate husband. This boy became a "man" all right, and quickly, but not because his father gave him The Blessing.

In movies, on TV, in essays written by my students, I've heard a lot of fathers tell their sons, "Ok, you're the man of the house now." Then they leave. Sometimes jobs take them away; sometimes death; sometimes other women; sometimes God; sometimes alcohol, drugs, dice. In my experience, though "You're the man of the house now" may sound like The Blessing, rarely, however, is it The Blessing.

In my experience, most men leave because they are Unblessed sons themselves. Their own father-hole, father-hunger calls them to fill up somewhere else. They had no Blessing to pass on; no idea how to give The Blessing to their own sons and daughters. They leave angry, ashamed, afraid, sad. Fatherhood has failed them just like their own fathers had failed them.

Somebody needs to be the man of the house. A house is not a home without a man. A boy can't be Blessed without a man around.

Somebody needs to begin The Blessing. Then the Blessed son has something to pass on. Blessing begets Blessing…

Son, I'm so sorry I left. I'm sorry for the pain my leaving caused you. I'm sorry that my own need for love won out over your need for love. I'm here now, I'm not going anywhere. And please don't allow what I did to hide this essential truth, a truth that was just as true the day I left, and every day since: You have all you need to be a strong and loving man. All you need to be the man of your house.

Salvation Son

I know a man whose father regarded him as his "Salvation Son." Having fathered a first son who was gay and then three daughters, his second son would do all the masculine things a son should do—and thereby prove his *father's* masculinity, save his *father's* manhood.

And this second son attempted to do just that. Handsome and strong, he excelled in sports and courted pretty women. There was a bout of mischievous adolescent rebellion where the son tried to assert his individuality, but for more than forty years, it's mostly been "Salvation Son" to the rescue: his own manhood on hold, his anger buried, his sadness disguised by Nice Guy, he has lived out his father's idea of what a man should be. He has lived for his father's praise, however perverted.

"My father never got tired of telling people how proud he was of me," this son said, through tears.

Of course, this is not The Blessing. This is another variation of The Curse. We sons will do anything to win our father's praise; we will even sacrifice our own manhood in order to save our fathers' manhood.

Son, I'm deeply, deeply sorry that I used you in order to make me feel more like a man. You are your own man, full of power and love. That is what I am proud of, and my only wish for you is for you to feel that power and love in your life. I bless the man I see in you.

Pete Nice

One of my roomies in grad school was this guy from Detroit who bestowed an MC name on anybody he cared about. One late night Dave knocked on my door to borrow a CD. I had been asleep, but I got up without a word, found the music, and gave it to him. As I was closing the door, he turned back, tapping the CD with one finger. "I gots your new handle, man," he said. "Pete Nice. Yeah. Pete Nice. Because you're just NICE, man, 24/7, know what I mean?"

I knew exactly what he meant. I'd been perfecting Pete Nice for close to thirty years. It was who I was. 24/7.

Pete Nice didn't get angry. Pete Nice didn't get loud. Pete Nice didn't get dirty. Pete Nice always listened. Pete Nice was always punctual. Pete Nice was always polite. Pete Nice always put the needs of girl friends, roommates, students, the world ahead of his own needs....

Pete Nice was a punk!

One of my dearest friends is a Nice Guy too. Today on the phone he told me that while he was growing up, his mother was always quietly telling him how to be in the world: *Don't be selfish, Don't be loud, Don't be late...*

"She wasn't intending to mess me up," he said, "but what happened was I took all this in and drew a circle around myself. This Nice Guy circle. And for most of my life I've been terrified to take a step outside of it—that if I did, I would hurt my mother in some way."

Don't get me wrong. Growing up, Nice worked for me, and for my friend too. It was the persona we unconsciously adopted to survive and to get as many of our needs met as possible. We were taught to be Nice by our mothers and fathers—and Nice was rewarded. And for those of us who weren't very big or aggressive, Nice was safe; Nice could stop you from getting punched in the nose.

I think there was something else going on here, too. Neither my friend nor I were shown a different way for a boy to be in the world. We both stood in our mother's circle, and we needed some sort of initiation—a ceremony led by strong, loving older men—to free us from our Niceness and to honor our authenticity as males.

Son, I honor you for being sensitive to the needs of others. But you also have your own wants and needs, and it's OK to speak them and to satisfy them. To do so doesn't make you 'not nice'; it makes you authentic. Strong, loving men do both: we are sensitive to the needs and wants of others, **and** *to our own wants and needs. And don't worry, you have all it takes to be a strong, loving man.*

Poor Me!

Poor me, my job sucks.

Poor me, I don't have any money.

Poor me, I don't have any friends.

Poor me, my wife and my boss are always telling me what to do.

Poor me, my mother, my father, my kids, my dog, my brother, my doctor, my neighbor, my paper boy, my shoes…are making me miserable.

I *hate* the Poor Me in me. I *hate* playing the whiny Victim.

No, that's not quite true: I *love* the Poor Me in me, too. I *love* my whiny Victim.

When I'm singing my Poor Me, I'm a boy crying out, *Take care of me, be there for me, meet my deep needs.* I'm a scared, sad boy silently screaming, *Bless me! Bless me! Somebody give me The Blessing! Tell me…*

Son, I see how much pain you're in and how powerless you feel. I'm here to remind you of your true strength. I'm right here to look you in the eyes and tell you Poor Me is not all of who you are; you are more than a Victim. You have all you need to step away from your scared, sad boy for a moment and step into the power of the Warrior within you. You have all the strength and love you need to take care of that boy, to be there for him, to meet his deep needs. To Bless him, and to Bless other scared, sad boys just like him.

My Little Boy

Several years ago, I bought myself a card with a little boy on the front. He's in maroon knickers, one pant leg rolled up, with a wave of soft brown hair leaking out from under a teal blue wool hat. Eyes closed, beatific smile, his whole head is tilted slightly toward the daisy he's holding in his right hand—and that's why I imagine his left hand is spread wide across his chest: the daisy, its ten-petaled yellow magnificence, its summer scent, is warming this little boy's heart.

When my wife, Julia, saw this card, she told me it was exactly right. "That's you—that's how I imagine your Little Boy."

She was talking about the glorious, pristine part of me unbesmirched by the wear and tear of the adult world; the part of me magnificently connected to the song and dance of the planet; the part of me hot-wired to play, wide open to play, infused by play. My Little Boy.

For much of my life, my Little Boy has been in hiding. Lost somewhere. Afraid to come out. Kidnapped. Stamped on the back of a milk carton. Run away. Sick. Imprisoned.

It happens to a lot of Little Boys. They get slapped, ignored, mannered, warned, teased, taunted, graded, rewarded, demoted, diminished, finished. Men see a kid holding a flower—they holler, "Put that god damn flower down, you pansy!" Doctors see a kid running around with the light of the world in his eyes and the play of the gods in his legs—and they Ridlin him. Kids sense all the secret sadness and shame and fear of adults—and their joy sinks.

It appears to be nearly impossible to have a healthy Little Boy in a world of stressed-out, emotionally challenged adults. Adults whose own Little Boys and Little Girls are sick or lost or imprisoned.

What does a man feel like when his Little Boy is alive and well? He feels like, well, a little boy: not childish, but childlike. He has stretches of time—seconds, minutes, hours—where "playful" is his password…where the world is so suddenly and utterly magical, the only thing he could do is jump up and jitterbug or burp or belt out "Rocky Mountain High" or "It's your birthday! It's your birthday!" even when it's not close to his birthday…Where the snow he's shoveling glistens like chips of diamond and the cardinal against the winter white is heart-stopping red…Where a banana split tastes like a gourmet dinner and the smell of mud instantly spring-cleans his spirit.

When my father wrestled and barked with the dogs on the family room floor—that was his Little Boy. When my cousin Mike leaps off a 90-foot platform with a five-year-old boy, and they both bungee-boomerang back up into the sky, squealing with delight—that's Mike's Little Boy. When Glenn and I danced like crazy, uninhibited fools, like deranged dervishes, while the summer rain poured down—that was our Little Boys.

Little Boys need to feel safe. If they feel safe, they come out and play. If they can't play, they begin to die. And if our Little Boy is dying, we're dying too; our joy is drying up, we're played out. It's that simple.

We men can choose to ignore that. Or deny it. Or maybe we are so disconnected from our Little Boy we believe he doesn't exist, or is dead. We might use alcohol or drugs to momentarily free our Little Boy. We might instinctively know that there is so much pain around our Little Boy that we will do anything, *any*thing, to avoid that pain. We might be crushingly afraid to bring our Little Boy out into a world that doesn't seem to cherish Little Boys.

Or we can dangle a lifeline to our Little Boy, create some safe space, offer him a Blessing.

Little Boy, I'm terribly sad and sorry that you've been in hiding for so long. I need you in my life. I am as serious as a disease, and your passion for play is my cure. Come out, come out, wherever you are! I promise you a safe space and any toy your heart desires.

BLESSING THE INITIATION OF MEN

Driving

My father always drove. My mom rode shotgun, my brother Paul behind her, my sister Robin in the middle, and me, the oldest, directly behind my father.

When I turned sixteen, my father taught me to drive. On sweet summer evenings, we went around the neighborhood in my mom's red-and-white VW van. My father was more relaxed than I expected; his instructions, as always, were brilliantly clear, but on these twilight drives, his words felt warmer and softer than usual.

On the day of my test, my father offered me his Benz. "It'll be easier to do your parallel parking," he said, and handed me the keys.

I passed on my first attempt. If I thought things were going to change in a big way, I was wrong: my father always still drove, my mom beside him, my brother behind her, my sister beside me, and me, with my fresh new license, directly behind my father.

It would be more than twenty years before I was again the driver and my father the passenger....

We were coming from Georgia, just the two of us, heading back to his home in Salem, South Carolina. We had gone to Atlanta to pick up his medical records. He wasn't doing great, having more and more trouble breathing, feeling weaker. But of course, he was still driving.

Thirty miles ago, he had been talking to me about my mother. "You know," he said, "she's more beautiful to me today than when I first met her." He had first met her nearly 50 years ago, when they were both in high school. And those words were some of the most beautiful I had ever heard my father speak. I was almost asleep now, remembering those words, finally slipping into a summer afternoon's nap after fighting it for as long as I could.

The car's gravelly stop jarred me back toward consciousness.

"I need to rest," my father said. "Can you drive?"

I was instantly alert, ready. I remember touching his shoulder as we crossed paths in the back of the car. The changing of the guard. A blessing.

I drove the rest of the way home while my father slept.

When I Became a Man (at 42)

In America, when and how and by whom is a boy initiated into manhood? With his confirmation or Bar Mitzvah? How about Boy Scouts? When he passes his driving test? Magically on his 18th birthday? His first beer, his first sexual experience, his first Varsity football game? Going off to college? Joining a fraternity or the military? His first "real" job?

I made my confirmation at 12; I passed my driver's test at 16; I made it to my 18th birthday. I drank beer, I had sex, I played sports, I went off to college—I even joined a frat. And after all that, I got a real job. These were rites of passage, yes, but they were hollow ones for me. Nowhere, in any of those possible initiations, did I feel like a boy becoming a man.

So, right through college, and, I have some shame in saying, for approximately two decades after, I remained an uninitiated boy. On the outside, I was a man with a Master's degree, a good job, a house, a car, a girl friend, friends—and on the inside, buried so deep that for years I could dodge it and even fool myself, I was a boy.

In many other cultures, especially in so-called "primitive" societies, boys between the ages of eleven and fifteen are much more clearly initiated into adulthood. As James Hollis details in *Under Saturn's Shadow: The Wounding and Healing of Men*, in what may seem to us cruel rituals—knocking out a tooth or clipping off an ear—a group of men in the community take the responsibility of breaking the hold of the mother's world, and introducing a boy to the spirit and culture of manhood. The whole process might take several days, or several weeks, and involve not only some sort of symbolic wounding, but also song and dance and vision quest. The boy returns to his community with badges on his body and images in his heart that are deep, permanent reminders that he has crossed over the threshold of boyhood into adulthood. He is a man, and he knows he's a man because he feels that in his skin and spirit.

Where is our group of men, fathers, elders willing and able to bestow the necessary wounding and blessing that will transform us from boys to men? Should boot camp, or Wall Street, or prison, or the NBA be our best options?

My father's death ignited my own initiation into manhood. But rather than the loving presence of a group of men, it was the sudden absence of one man that inflicted my necessary wounding; and I wasn't 12 or 14—I was nearly 39. I was then on my own again for the next three years, until my New Warrior weekend in 2001.

On that weekend, I was initiated into manhood by a group of strong, loving men. On my forty-second birthday, thirty years overdue, I finally became a man.

Son, I'm sorry you had to wait so long before entering the community of men. I honor your courage in stepping into the fire of initiation. I celebrate your birth day; I bless your manhood; I believe in your love and your strength.

Coaches

I had bad luck with coaches. One was a walking temper tantrum. One was a racist. One was spitting crazy. One was a bully. Only the first and last—my eighth-grade basketball coach and my college varsity basketball coach—were guys I respected.

And most of the coaches I've observed since have been less than glorious. I saw Bobby Knight head-butt one of his players. I've seen a hundred coaches turn red from screaming. Throw things. Cuss. Turn away utterly disgusted. Coaches whose relationship skills stopped at public shaming.

I realize my assessment is distorted because most of the coaches I'm talking about are at big-time sports programs making big-time money with big-time pressures. I, however, played ball at a small Division III school, a school prized not for its athletics but for its academics. And my high school was just like thousands of other middle-sized suburban high schools. I would expect that at places like this there would be coaches worthy of respect.

What I got, however, were abusive, power-tripping boys.

What did I want? Coaches who cared more about their players' physical and psychological health than about a won-lost record and their ego. Coaches who realized that, for many boys, they are father figures. Coaches, then, who were strong, loving men capable of supplementing a father's role—who, instead of cursing and hollering, instead of suck-it-up and "no pain, no gain," could Bless, and thereby truly, powerfully, and lovingly help initiate boys into manhood.

As a basketball player, I overpassed, was too unselfish—afraid to look for my shot, afraid to assert myself. When harassed by a coach, things got worse—I was stiff and reckless. I rode myself hard enough; I didn't need somebody else riding me, shaming me, especially someone I didn't respect.

Here's what I wished I had heard from at least one of my coaches:

Peter, I love you for your unselfishness—you're a brilliant passer. But it's OK to look for your own shot. It's OK to be in the spotlight every once in a while. More than anything, though, I just want you to enjoy yourself out there. Enjoy the game. When you're having fun, you have a natural grace, a fluidity. Everything else takes care of itself.

The specifics of The Blessing would vary from player to player. But the essence, the spirit would be the same:

Son, enjoy the game, enjoy your innate strength and grace, enjoy your growth. Everything else is secondary.

My Vietnam

Growing up, I felt like Vietnam was my war just as surely as WWII was my father's war. And I was scared shitless—and fascinated at the same time.

The nightly news terrified me: Angry helicopters; muddy, twisted bodies bouncing around on stretchers; the thick fountain of blood spraying from the other side of that man's head; naked, napalmed children. And ping-pong balls—ping-pong balls with birth dates painted on them. I had horrible dreams where bloody red stitches spelled "June 23," my birthday, across the blank white face of a ping-pong ball.

And despite all that horror, I was drawn to the war. I had already felt the teamwork of sports, of boys rallying around each other to win the game; war was the next level—men rallying around each other to dodge death, to win freedom. And all the Saturday afternoon John Wayne and Audie Murphy movies I suffered through just to be close to my dad confirmed that: war was the ultimate initiation, a holy place where boys go to become men.

But I was a coward. I didn't want to go into that dark swampy jungle. I didn't want to lose a leg, I didn't want to die. But surely I was going, would have to go. My cousin Chris was already there, already wounded, shrapnel permanently embedded in his leg. And his buddy in front of him who stepped on the mine—already dead.

I was a ten-year-old boy tossing and turning in my bed while the 11 o'clock news blared below, a boy absolutely petrified of doing the one and only thing he could see that would make him a man.

I don't remember if my father was for or against the war; I don't remember him ever telling me he expected me to go to war in order to win my manhood. I don't think he had to. Despite the deepening anti-war sentiment, where I was growing up in upstate New York, the air was heavy with fathers who had fought heroically against Hitler. The voices of those fathers—and of countless fathers throughout the war-torn ages—talked to me constantly, telling me what I had to do if I was going to measure up. Fathers telling their sons that going to war would win them The Blessing.

"I went to war to show my father I was worthy," says Vietnam vet Jeff Duvall in a recent interview in *The New Warrior Journal*, "that I was a man he should love. My attempts to gain my father's love and approval failed…even going to war was not enough for my father to bless me."

Thankfully, I never had to go. The war ended when I was 14. And I know Duvall is right, that going to war will not automatically win a father's love. Still, part of me felt like I'd been cheated. Vietnam was my war, and I had lost my best chance at earning my manhood, at winning The Blessing.

Son, you don't have to go to war to prove you're a man. You don't have to go to war to gain my love. You have my love now, and you have all you need to be a strong, loving man. And a strong, loving man chooses his wars carefully. He understands the horror of war, and so he only fights when his heart tells him it is right to fight. And then he fights with all his strength.

Birth & War

I've been reading books and talking to people about what my pregnant wife will go through in five months. One strapping, athletic father in Kids R Us told me, "After I saw what my wife went through to give birth to our first boy—Honey, I said to her, anything you want, I'll do anything you want. It was absolutely unbelievable."

The incredible, indescribable pain of labor. I'm wondering if giving birth is the ultimate initiation for many women. Yes, menstruation tells women that they bleed, and there is sometimes even severe cramping that comes with it. But, my god, giving birth—hours and hours of pushing a seven- or eight- or nine-pound baby out of your belly and into the world! That's not the play of girls—that is the strength of warrior women. I suspect any residual innocence is sacrificed, replaced by a visceral understanding that birth and death are inseparably close, that suffering is a necessary part of creation—and I, a woman, cannot only endure it, I'm a vital participant in it.

Does a man have an equivalent experience? Is there any kind of comparable initiation where a man undergoes sufficient, sustained pain to shed his illusions of innocence, of purity, of immortality—of all the ideas that define him as a boy?

War. When a boy goes off to war. War has traditionally been a male's labor—a place he went off to to protect the women and children, to birth his warrior, to shed his boyhood and return a man. The only problem with this scenario is, instead of bringing life into the world, a new baby, he has often been forced to destroy life—even kill babies. So many men have come back crippled, stunted, disconnected. Their innocence had been blown away, yes, war had accomplished that; but it had been replaced with shame and fear and anger and sadness. They were no longer sweet boys—they were embittered old men.

Other than war, what new initiations can men enact that will deliver us from our boyhood without destroying our spirit? What new ceremonies can men create that will enable us to surrender our illusions of purity and immortality—and thereby anchor us to the wonderful, immense responsibilities we have on this nitty-gritty earth—without robbing us of our soul? How can we men become spiritual warriors without going off to war?

Big, big questions. Maybe we can begin with a Blessing.

Men, I honor you for honoring the labor of women. You desperately want to be as strong and loving a man as you see in the strength and love of this woman giving birth. I tell you now that you already have that strength and love inside you, just as the woman does; and it is your job to create profoundly challenging, spiritual ceremonies with other men to honor your strength and love. The first time you were born by the strength and love of women—this second time you shall be born by the strength and love of men.

Kill Your Mother, Marry Your Father

That's going to be the title of my next book: *Kill Your Mother, Marry Your Father.* If we don't, we end up like Oedipus. Oedipus got it backwards, poor guy: he killed his father, married his mother.

You're probably well acquainted with Freud's Oedipal Complex: we sons will fight our father for the right to make love to our mother. Motherfucker wannabes, apparently, all of us, and that's completely normal at a young age. But we need a counter-force to the pull toward mother—and that's the pull of father. And at some crucial age, say twelve to fourteen, a clean, clear separation from the mother—an initiation by men into manhood—is developmentally necessary.

"Kill your Mother, Marry your Father" is one way to describe what must happen in that initiation. The boy must "kill" his mother: He must summon enough masculine energy to cut the umbilical cord, once and for all. He acquires this strength by "marrying" his father: by embracing the masculine energy embodied in his father. If the father isn't there—if he's abandoned us, or we've killed him off somehow—things get ugly and stunted. Without the necessary masculine energy, the son's psyche fails to develop; he remains attached to his mother's world. He stays a boy.

Actually, it's even trickier than that, and here is where my "Kill your mother" is clearly overkill. For as Terrence Real points out in *I Don't Want To Talk About It,* male initiations too often just continue the toughening-up process that starts for boys at birth: the ritual wounds are often physically abusive, and they are frequently accompanied by mocking and shaming. The result for boys is further disconnection from the "emotional and relational richness that is their birthright." In my idea of initiation, a father invites the boy out of his mother's circle and into a circle of men who, without assaulting or shaming, can teach him how to be both strong *and* loving.

The Blessing can accompany and assist a boy's initiation. If given, he is freed not only from carrying out Oedipus' horrible and literal crimes of murder and incest, but also from the often-devastating *psychological* manifestations of father-rage and emotional incest. It reassures a boy that he has all it takes to become a man—the strength and the love.

Son, you're ready now. You are ready to leave the world of mothers and enter the world of men. I won't lie to you: this will hurt. You may even feel like you're dying, and maybe as if you're killing your mother. She's OK. She's a strong woman. She understands this is a necessary step in your becoming a man and supports it, and you, wholeheartedly. We both know you have all it takes to be a strong, loving man. And we are both proud of you for choosing to undergo this pain in order to step into your power.

Umbilical Cord

My umbilical cord has been cut twice: the first time on June 23, 1959 by some doctor in Schenectady, NY; the second time on June 23, 2001, my forty-second birthday, by me in Wallaceburg, Ontario.

I don't remember that first time. What I remember of the second time is working my way through a birth canal of ten or twelve men, fighting my way toward the light; getting caught up half-way through and having to slow down, gather myself. And at the end, naked, breathing hard, cutting through a thick rope with a plastic knife. I cut furiously, powered by anger, determination, joy. When the last sliver of rope broke, I was finally free. A man.

The first time, I was born from a woman. The second time, from men. The first time I was small and helpless, barely conscious; the second time, I was empowered and fully awake. I had made a decision. I was finally ready to leave my childhood behind and to be born again as a man.

That second birth was thirty years overdue. Ideally, it would have happened when I was about twelve, on the cusp of manhood. My father would have taken me from my mother and led me to a group of men—friends, elders, grandfathers. They would have spoken their truth as men, Blessed me, and initiated me. Cut from my boyhood, I would have returned a man.

It's happened all over the world for thousands of years: Men birthing men.

One of the men who lead me through my second birthing later told me he wasn't sure I would be able to cut through the rope with that plastic knife. "But you went at it with so much energy...thirty seconds later, done!"

After, I rested. They put a blanket over me, I chose a man to hold me, and I rested.

I've never felt so relaxed and alive in all my life.

BLESSING OUR HEROES

Arnie's Army

"*Arnold?*" *the priest's eyes questioned.*

You were supposed to choose a saint for your confirmation name, and it was obvious Arnold wasn't ringing any saintly bells.

"*As in Palmer,*" *I said.*

The priest nodded. In 1971, even priests knew who Arnold Palmer was—and maybe, like me, thought Arnie was capable of miracles.

My dad and I were part of Arnie's Army. We watched him on our big Zenith, waiting for his inevitable "Charge!" His arms and face were bronzed by a lot of golf course sun; he had Paul Newman brown hair and a shy smile. When he strode down the fairway he would occasionally hitch his pants up over his snaky hips, sometimes puffing no-hands on a cigarette. Arnie didn't swing at a golf ball—he lashed at it, following it with an angry twist of his club like a guy with a divining stick searching hysterically for water. His putting stroke was more slapshot than sweet spot: knees knocked, arms locked, he willed the ball into the hole—and grimaced like a shot man if it lipped out.

His nemesis was Jack Nicklaus, younger by a decade, a puffy blond crew-cutter with a picture-perfect, powerful golf swing. I hated Jack (Fat Jack, I called him, right to the TV's face); he was unflappable flab and not enough flair. And worse, he was too good; he beat Arnie too many Sundays.

Thirty years later, I see all too clearly whom I was rooting for on all those Sundays when I thought I was cheering on Arnie: I was rooting for my father. Like Arnie, my father's golf swing was all will and no grace; picking up the game at 28, he developed a tight, rapid, slashy swing that one of his friends dubbed "Zorro." And like Arnie, my dad was the gritty underdog to the likes of Eddie O'Keefe and Art Hemker, smooth-swingers born with silver golf clubs in their hands. When I caddied for my father, I got a rare close-up of both his incredible courage and his incessant self-doubt. More often than not, he was out of his league, in over his head—or so he felt—and all he could do was grip the driver even tighter, pop it down the middle, steel will it onto the green, and cross-hand rap it, somehow, into the hole.

I was there on the fifteenth green, the flag in my hand, when his thirty-foot birdie putt dropped, closing out Dr. O'Keefe and moving my father into the finals of the

Mohawk Club Championship. I was sixteen years old, and I was so proud of my father I felt tears swell up and take over my eyes. I wanted to hug him, but all I could do was slap him on the back again and again.

Last year, I watched Arnold Palmer walk up the eighteenth fairway at Augusta for his fiftieth and last time. In his mid-seventies now, his legs hurting, the "Charge" all discharged, he walks like an old man. And for the first time I sensed a sadness he has carried with him all these years. That's another thing Arnie and my dad shared, this deep life-long sadness—that, and an old warrior's will to ignore that sadness, and that fear, and all that self-doubt, and to find a way, somehow, to prevail.

And when I write that, I feel proud all over again, and I feel my own sadness, and I wish my father were here so we could talk about that brilliant birdie day back in 1975, his courage, and maybe his self-doubt, and mine, and I could finally hug him for all of it. For all of it.

Amen.

What do Tiger and Michael and Lance Have in Common?

They are driven sons. I feel the presence and absence of father in every shot they take, every hill they attack.

There is something in their eyes and demeanor, an insatiable hardness. Pete Rose had it too, and so did another Pete, Pistol Pete Maravich, although there was a sadness in his eyes as well.

I admit to knowing very little about the fathers of these athletes. I do know that Press Maravich and Harry Rose were hard-nosed, driven athletes themselves, that Lance's father was conspicuously absent and Tiger's father a formidable presence. But I am the driven son of a driven son. Like the sons of alcoholics, I can pick out other sons with my disease.

I admire these athletes for their talent, their competitiveness, their intensity. I am awed by their discipline and determination. But I feel some sadness, too, when I think of them. And anger. And shame.

I am angry because I sense that their fathers always wanted more, and more, and more. That their fathers never told them enough was enough, that they could rest now. Retire even.

I am angry that this society so frantically applauds their "drive," their "gamesmanship," their "competitiveness" without questioning whether it's gone too far. Without looking at the source. Without considering what is lost or missing when someone is so obsessed with winning.

And I am ashamed, strange as it may sound, that I was not this kind of son for my own father—a son driven enough, and talented enough, to earn my father's love. To earn The Blessing.

My father was just beginning to get ill when Tiger won the Masters in 1997 by twelve strokes. An excellent golfer himself, a student of the game, my father was awestruck by the magnitude of Tiger's win. I saw it in his eyes. I had never seen the same look for anything I had accomplished.

If I could win the Masters, I could win his love. If I could score 44 points a game, like Pistol Pete, I could win his love. If I could write a best-selling novel, I could win his love.

If I could do anything "Great," I believed I would earn The Blessing from my father.

These athletes, these sons *have* done something "great," and yet their eyes tell me, their words tell me, their relentless action tells me they have not received The Blessing. They have not received the peace—the sense of "good enough"—The Blessing brings.

And it is this ceaseless restlessness that pricks my sadness.

When will a father or a father figure or an elder or a powerful, heart-driven man look us in the eyes and tell us:

Son, you don't need another hit, another hoop, a higher test score, a higher-paying job. Right now, with all you have accomplished and all you haven't accomplished, you are good enough. Man enough. You can rest.

Pistol Pete

I've never quite forgiven my mother for falling asleep late at night just before giving birth to me. As a result, instead of being born on June 22 like my hero, Pistol Pete Maravich, I was born in the early hours of June 23.

No, "hero" isn't quite the right word: Pete Maravich was my older brother, my namesake. My alter ego. Pete was skinny like me. Pete had a father like mine—big heart, big expectations, bigger-than-life. And from the first time I ever saw him throw a no-look-around-the-back-pass at LSU, I had a strong, strange feeling that our lives were connected and we were playing for the same thing: our father's Blessing.

Years later, I said it this way in a poem:

Pistol Pete

> I didn't have your flyaway hair
> but I had your stringy limbs
> and floppy unhappy socks
> and the same burning need
> to win my father's love
> with one
> > unimaginably
> > > magical
> > > > pass.

Neither one of us ever threw such a magical pass, at least not on the basketball court. When hoop failed, we looked to other things to fill up our hole. Pete tried beer, karate, Christianity; I tried literature, politics, Buddhism. We kept searching, stayed sad.

Then our fathers got sick. These once invincible men of ours lay dying. We stayed by their side, no longer so obsessed with getting The Blessing. Just happy to be close to them, to be needed by them. When our fathers died, I was 38, Pete was 39, and he would die himself just eight months later.

Recently, my friend Brendan sent me an article from the *NY Times* about one of Pete's sons. He's played ball at five different colleges, has had more than his share of serious injuries, but he can't let it go—the dream that one day he'll throw that unimaginably magical pass and his father, Pistol Pete Maravich, will give him The Blessing from the other side of the grave.

Son, you can stop now. The day you were born, the moment I saw your head crown was more beautiful, more magical than any around-the-back-through-the-legs-over-the-shoulder-off-the-elbow-no-look pass I've ever seen in my life. You are a powerful, loving man. You are enough. You can rest in peace.

Jesus, Brother

Growing up in a house where my father was God, I empathized with Jesus. I knew first-hand how hard it was to be a son of God.

I can see Jesus, at maybe thirteen or fourteen, talking wisdom to the wise men. I never would have said it aloud, could barely think it, but I believed I sometimes knew more about truth and beauty than God my father.

I can see Jesus smashing tables and cracking heads in the temple. Somewhere deep inside me, I wanted to do the same thing—let all my righteous anger out. But God my father would have done some of his own head cracking if I had.

I can see Jesus alone in the desert suffering the Devil's temptations of power. My bedroom was my desert, and while God my father watched TV downstairs, me and the Devil went one-on-one.

I can hear Jesus being Blessed by his Father: "You are my son, whom I love; with you I am well pleased." I craved the same Blessing from God my father.

I can hear Jesus cry out on the cross, "My God, my God, why hast thou forsaken me?" At night, nailed by fear and hope to my bed, I've uttered the same cry to God my father.

I don't know if Jesus is the Son of God. I do know he, like me, is a son of a hard-to-please, powerful father; a son who tried with all his heart to be worthy of his father's love.

And for this, as for any son who has endured a godly father, I call him my brother.

The Woods Beyond my Father's House

Mr. Z said you close the door to your classroom, and it's your world. Ken said you make a revolution, and you change the whole world.

These two men changed me forever. I was emerging from college, looking for something big to do with my life; something with some meaning. My father's life, as accomplished as it was, wasn't for me. I had no interest in business, and at the time, no interest in settling down and having a family. There was this whole, huge world out there, and I wanted to explore it and heal it. But I needed some guidance. I needed a couple of intelligent, passionate men to lead me through the woods beyond my father's house.

Richard Zagrandski, a.k.a. Mr. Z, is still, twenty-five years later, the best teacher I have ever seen. He loved his students, fifteen boys from all sorts of backgrounds who were repeating high school English class that summer, and they loved him right back. When they came in in the morning, Mr. Z would be tipped back in his chair, feet up on the desk, drinking his coffee, smiling, truly happy as hell to see them, to joke with them, to listen to them. And he taught the same way: joking, talking, moving, questioning, listening. He made these "remedial" students forget they were "dumb"; for him, they were full of ideas, full of stories, full of life. Sure, they needed help with their skills, and he helped them; but they already had the important things—good heads, good hearts.

After those six summer weeks as a teaching assistant with Mr. Z, I called Columbia grad school and told them I would not be coming in the fall. To hell with scholarship, I wanted to teach! I wanted to close my classroom door and see if I could create some of my own magic.

I met Ken four years later. I was disillusioned at the time—not with teaching, as I had had two wonderful years at a prep school finding out I could do some of what Mr. Z did in a classroom, but with grad school. Was this it? Would I spend the rest of my life closing my classroom door and teaching literature in some privileged, little world? That had been my dream, but now it felt too small and selfish. It had come to my awareness there were thousands of nuclear weapons out there, millions of unemployed, billions of hungry people. What was I going to do about all that?

Ken was attacking all that head-on. He was a revolutionary. And that doesn't mean he was crazy or ready to blow shit up. He loved people, and it hurt him to see what this system was doing to them. His eyes told me that. And he loved ideas, believed in the power of ideas and the power of his own mind.

I spent the next four months pondering radical politics with him. Ken would drive in from Detroit and meet me in some coffee place in Ann Arbor, or we'd stake out a booth in the University of Michigan student center. He presented revolution, communism, dialectical materialism—and I listened, questioned, read. I grew to trust him. Like Mr. Z, he was a great teacher—patient, creative, committed. In my judgment, he was more of an intellectual—and less of a hypocrite—than my grad school professors: He was willing to thoroughly examine a set of ideas that most American "intellectuals" wouldn't even touch, and he was willing to act on the consequences of those ideas. I admired his courage, his love, and his intelligence.

When I was convinced, and he was convinced I was convinced, I joined him and a small group of other revolutionaries who valued these ideas and wanted to see a world run for the interests of people, not profit. I was a committed revolutionary for the next eight years of my life.

Although they didn't initiate me directly into manhood, these two middle-aged men opened up new worlds for me, initiated me into the worthy professions of teaching and revolution. They were models for what intelligent, loving men could do in the world. When Mr. Z closed his classroom door, he created a different world for those teen-age boys, a world where they were heard and respected. He treated these teens as I had wanted to be treated as a teen. And when Ken listened to my questions, took them seriously, took ideas seriously, and the consequences of ideas; when he risked his vision of a brave, new world, I felt heard and enthralled. Unlike most adults, he treated me like the serious truth-seeking young man I was.

These two men mentored me, blessed me through my twenties.

Son, I see you are hungry to make this a better world. I honor you for using your mind and following your heart, even when your ideas and feelings lead you to unconventional places. You are a strong, loving man who is doing his best to create a strong, loving world.

Malcolm X

The only memory I have from 1965, the year Malcolm X was assassinated, is my father and I watching Jim Brown catch a little screen pass and power his way upfield for the last time in his career. But in the late 1980s, I read Malcolm's autobiography and all his speeches, and watched every film and documentary I could get my hands on.

Malcolm mesmerized me. I loved his quick tongue, his darting eyes, his disarming smile. I loved when he went to Harvard and defeated all the tweed-coated professors in debate. I loved his absolute passion and his infinite loyalty. I loved the courage he had to admit he had been wrong and to change his path, even though he knew that to do so meant his life. In his eulogy, Ossie Davis said, "Malcolm was our manhood, our living, black manhood!" And that's how I, a thirty-year-old white man, felt about Malcolm: Finally, here was a man, here was a living, loving, powerful man!

There is so much about Malcolm's story that touched and triggered parts of my story:

Like me, he was the Good Son—until his father was murdered by the Klu Klux Klan and his mother was institutionalized.

Like me, he was a son who had been hurt, and like me, he was angry about being hurt—but unlike me, he spoke his anger. I loved Malcolm's righteous, eloquent vehemence: although his vitriol was often directed at the white men in power and the way black men and women were unjustly treated in America, I unconsciously felt he was speaking of the way I had been unjustly treated by a powerful white man, my father.

Like me, he was actively, if unconsciously, searching for a "second" father, and found him for a time in the form of Elijah Muhammad. And in one sense, Malcolm was *my* second father, my "black" father, my shadow father. Killed when I was five, Malcolm could safely carry all the heavy projections I threw on him; he could be all the things my father wasn't: urban, worldly, heroic, dead. I was fascinated by Harlem; my father was terrified of Harlem; Malcolm *was* Harlem.

But since my father's death, I have come to realize how much Malcolm and my father actually had in common: their sharp wit, their good looks, their charismatic strength, their underlying sadness. Unable to fully embrace these qualities in my own father, I projected them on to Malcolm—and worshipped him.

My present work is to own Malcolm's gold, and my father's gold, as my own. And in so doing, I no longer want to *be* Malcolm; I want to be like him. A lost, Unblessed son himself, he made it his life's mission to bless all of Harlem's lost sons, of whom I am but one of millions.

Malcolm, I honor your beautiful authenticity, your impeccable integrity, your undying curiosity. When I see you standing so tall and speaking with such loving strength, I see a model of manhood—of the man I am becoming.

Iron Robert

In early July of 1997, I got stranded for a day and a night in LaGuardia airport. I didn't care. I was leaving behind a taxing, toxic relationship and heading to Eastern Europe for a month of backpacking. I felt suddenly lighter at thirty-eight than I had in years, and my travel buzz was palpable. In that space, I pulled Robert Bly's *Iron John* out of my knapsack and felt it talking straight to me right from the "Preface"'s opening paragraph:

> By the time a man is thirty-five he knows that the images of the right man, the tough man, the true man which he received in high school do not work in life. Such a man is open to new visions of what a man is or could be.

Suddenly I was just such a man. Without quite realizing it, I was knee-deep in the early muck of a mid-life crisis. My images of what a man is, confused from the start, were fading fast, nearly played out. As far as what a man could be…in all my years of truth-searching, I had never framed the question in that way. I had no idea what a man could be. I was ripe for a new vision.

Bly's lucid sentences, his vivid mythmaking, his wise commentary were the initial brushstrokes of that new vision. I felt as if I had been trudging outside in a raging blizzard for decades, around and around and around, and had suddenly stumbled upon a storm door, wide open and welcoming. In a flash, I was in a warm basement, kicking my boots off, rubbing my raw feet, watching shadows play like movies across the wall…

There I was! The "soft male," the guy more in touch with his feminine than John Wayne ever was—"the nice boy who pleases not only his mother but also the young woman he is living with." Yes, that's me! That's me! Where was my warrior energy, where was the key to unlock my Wild Man?

Under my mother's pillow, said Bly! How did he know that, how the hell did he know that?! OK, Freud gave him a clue, but I had read some Freud, years before, and Freud never said it like this. All at once, *Iron John* felt so incredibly learned, so deep and so rich, so ancient, so poetic—so spot-on kitchen-table true.

Because there I was again! The hungry, high-flying son in the chapter, "The Hunger for the King in a Time with No Father." The son, like so many sons, Bly points out, who lost his father to the new configurations of work—the father who no longer farms, but disappears into the city, only to return at night tired out and pissed off. We are living in the times of Darth Vader, the dark father, and sons like me try to fly away toward the sun, toward enlightenment, toward achievement.

And there I was again, and again! Kitchen-helper and gardener, wound and Warrior. This book was not my life, exactly, but my inner life—the life I had only glimpsed in dreams and in surreal seconds. Bly, a lost son himself, introduced me to my lost father—to a boy being taught the dance of manhood by his father.

Fathers and sons have been doing this dance for thousands of years, I heard Bly saying. Right now, it was awkward, damn awkward. Not enough drums, not enough father. I felt that all too keenly, all too painfully. But this book meant I was not alone. I was a boy among boys, I was a son among sons, I was a man among men—curious, fearful, enraged, ashamed, sad, weak, heroic, lost, Wild, depressed.

I could live with that. I was even excited about that. Yes, we men were isolated, alienated, disconnected, all of us hidden in our own little world—but think of the reconciliation, the reunion, the joy were we to circle up, open up, and let some of our pain out and our power in! Bly gave me hope that I could someday grow up and join the community of men.

I met Robert last year at an International Men's Conference here in Detroit. He's got a mane of white hair and an elder's stature, but it's only the tiniest tremor in his stately voice when reciting poetry that hints he's nearly eighty. I liked him as much as I thought I would. He is passionate, political, prickly, funny. He feels like someone whose skin has been lived in, who has taken in the raw stuff of his life, the pulp and the pain and the joy, and squeezed out rich lines of poetry. He's a man who knows how big he is, and how small too; Bly is a mountain, and a ruby-throated hummingbird.

I want to be a wise man like Robert Bly when I grow up. I want to write a book about men as truthful and as beautiful as *Iron John*.

BLESSING OUR FAMILY

The Letter

Until the very last days of his life, the closest my father ever came to giving me The Blessing was the letter he sent me my first semester of college.

There was nothing earthshaking in that letter, no glorious words of praise, no shining fatherly advice. As best as I can remember, it was just mundane news—"How's school?" "Howie and I went hunting…," "I flew to Syracuse with your mother…"

But the point is, my father didn't write letters. My father didn't write, period. He might scribble a reminder on the back of an envelope or write out a check, but even that was rare: he kept most things in his head and paid cash every time he could. You had to sit down to write letters, sit still, reflect, maybe emote; my father's feet and mind were always moving forward, and emotions were an uncomfortable drag.

I knew all this. Even then, I knew who my father was. And because I was going to major in English, because I already loved to ferret out what a text was saying and then to write about it, I knew what this letter was saying beneath the day-to-day nothings. I heard the unspoken Blessing loud and clear:

Son, you did it, you're off on your own now! I don't even have the words to tell you how proud I am of you. How I miss you.

He had me with "Dear Petey." And by the end of the letter, my eyes were so tear-stained I could barely read the "Love, Dad."

I was taking a freshman seminar on autobiography, and our final paper was to write our own autobiography. After receiving his letter, it was suddenly clear to me that my life up to that point had been organized around winning my father's love. That's who I was: I was Peter Jr. doing everything I could to win Peter Sr.'s love. So that's what I wrote in that paper, using the letter and my reaction to it as my central piece of evidence.

The professor loved it, and so, I hope, did my father. But I'll never know for sure. Though I sent it to him, he never said anything about it. And I spent the next twenty-five years of my life still trying to win my father's love—nearly a quarter-century awaiting his next Blessed words.

"Son"

A beautiful word, "Son."

My father never called me "Son." He called me "Petey." As he was leaving the hospital the day his father died, BaPa, my grandfather, had said "Good-bye, Petey." When I came home for the funeral, my father said, "He hadn't called me Petey in forty years. I think he was saying good-bye to both of us."

Those two sentences were the most intimate words I had ever heard my father speak.

But he never called me "Son." I would have liked that. For me, "son" is the most intimate word in the English language. The most charged.

"Son" is the first word of The Blessing: "Son, you have all it takes..." Behind that "Son" is a man—a future father.

That's why it pierces my heart when Julia's seventh-grade boys call each other "Son." For them, it's about one-upmanship, about power—about who is the big bad Father: "*Son*, you better do what I say." "I'm not the son—*you're* the son."

These twelve-year-old boys pretending they are fathers. Thinking that what it means to be a father is power over another. Power over their sons. Unblessed sons themselves, how could they know how to give The Blessing?

Son, you have all it takes to be a man. You have all it takes to be a wonderful father: a father whose love is powerful and whose power is loving...and whose son will be glorious.

"Bro"

That's what my brother, Paul, usually calls me—"Bro." "Pete" every so often, but mostly "Bro." And I like it. It's way more intimate than, say, "Dude," and it's who we are. It speaks of our history together.

When you have a bad-ass father in the house, your brother can be your best friend, your best ally. Paul was that for me. We dug forts, caught frogs, threw Frisbees. And we had each other's backs when it came to Dad.

That arrangement worked beautifully for maybe the first ten years of my life and the first eight years of his. Playing with each other, protecting each other: Best friends, brothers. But then something happened. Not all at once, but slowly, gradually, we began to find separate ways of dealing with my father.

I was the Good Boy who always thought the next "A" or the next hoop was going to win my father's love.

And since Good Boy was taken, Paul played the Bad Boy who pretended he didn't care about winning my father's love, but hoped he might use his immense potential and mediocre grades to earn a little negative attention.

I think things stayed on that path until my father got sick. His illness brought us back together again. Here we were, now in our mid- and late-thirties, helping each other with the same man who caused us so much pain and confusion so many years ago.

After our father's death, Paul and I were forced to team up on some financial matters. We found our styles complemented each other: Paul has my Dad's off-the-cuff chutzpa; I'm the diplomatic, "worst-case" scenario guy.

But it is truly on my wedding day eighteen months ago that Paul proved beyond any doubt, that, until death do us part, he is my one and only brother. He did it all—set up, take down, here are the rings, can I get you some water, be quiet he's meditating, Bernie get the hell out of here...everything. And he did it joyously. It didn't feel like "have to" or "should"; it felt like want to and love.

Not too long after the wedding, we were having a discussion about men we respected. Julia asked Paul, "What men, if any, do you respect?" Without hesitating, my brother answered, "Bro, of course."

It was one of the greatest blessings of my life.

"Dude!"

My friend Jimmy was telling me a guy did some research on "Dude." He found it was a perfect word for men to refer to each other: it connects us—without triggering our homophobia.

Men want to be connected to other men. Men want to talk to other men. Men want to be around other men.

"Dude!"

But we men are also afraid of other men. We don't want to give even the tiniest hint that we may be "Gay!" "Homo!" "Queer!" "Faggot!" We don't want other men to know we have feelings like sadness, fear, or shame. We don't want other men to know we often feel alone, and small.

So: "Dude!"

We are a bunch of Dudes! Dude ranchers. Cowboys.

When a man gives another man a blessing, he doesn't begin it with "Dude." He says:

Jimmy, you are a strong, loving man. Call me "Dude," if you want to, but I am also a brother who cares about you; who honors both your strength and your fear, your joy and your sadness, your pride and your shame.

When a father gives his son The Blessing, he doesn't begin it with "Dude." He says:

Son, you are much more than a "Dude." Gay or straight, you have all you need to be a strong, loving man.

Uncles

Everybody I know has a messed-up uncle. When I say that to my students, they laugh; they have messed-up uncles too.

Even Hamlet has one. "Oh my prophetic soul! My uncle!" he cries, when he finds out his father's brother has killed his father and married his mother. He knew it all along—it had to be the messed-up uncle!

I've got a couple of messed-up uncles myself. One of them spent the last twenty years of his life pretending he had a job and was going to work. But I didn't mind Messed-up Uncle #1. I would sit in a chair at his house—he'd have his feet up, drinking a Highball, whatever the hell that was—and he and I would watch sports together. Just like I did with my father. And when I was twelve, he took us down to Madison Square Garden to watch the NIT. He wasn't afraid of NYC, which was about the only thing my father *was* afraid of. And I wasn't afraid of Messed-up Uncle #1 like I was of my father. I felt sorry for him. I had heard a whispered story that his brother was this great guy/genius and got all the attention growing up—that's why Messed-up Uncle #1 was the way he was. That made sense to me.

I don't know a thing about Messed-up Uncle #2's childhood. I just know he was a good-looking, very physical guy who needed to beat us in any game we played, and that he had left my aunt. I hadn't seen him in twenty years, and the first thing he said to me as I walked through the door at his son's wedding was, "Remember how I beat you in one-on-one the last time we played?" He still had that little kid gloat. "No," I said, "I don't." I was fifteen at the time, weighed maybe 120 lbs; he was a 180 lb. thirty-five-year-old. And when I did remember, I recall letting him win because it wasn't that important to me—and *extremely* important to him.

I'm an uncle myself now. The crazy, funny uncle. Uncle Sponge Bob Square Pants. I'm not job-challenged like Messed-up Uncle #1 or hyper-competitive like Messed-up Uncle #2. But some, until recently, might well have called me "messed-up," too. I was the forty-year old Peter Pan, the guy who was never going to grow up and have kids of his own. A kid himself. A boy, finally. An Unblessed boy. Just like my uncles.

Cousins

If you've got yourself some messed-up uncles, it's a sure thing you've got yourself some crazy cousins.

I've got one cousin who has found it a matter of life and death to launch himself thousands of times from high places—bridges, helicopters, buildings. I'm convinced that after each jump he's hoping his father will be waiting at the bottom—or at the top—to tell him he's proud, and that's enough. He can stop now.

I have several cousins who drink and drug themselves up. They party until the pain goes away for the day.

I have another cousin who has filled himself up with God the Father because his own father thought he was god.

I have still another cousin who was working himself to death at Father Corporation so he could be the provider to his children his father never was.

Why all this craziness?

Why can't my cousins stop, why don't they feel they're enough?

Because their fathers couldn't stop, their fathers didn't feel they were enough. Because their fathers did not or would not or could not give them The Blessing.

My cousins, can you hear me through your sad, angry, crazy pain? You are beautiful men, strong and loving. Can you hear that? You don't have to prove a thing to anybody—not to your own father or your own children, not to the boy next door, or the guy in the bar, or the boss behind the desk. Not even to yourself. You are man enough right now. Can you stop and rest in that?

Dean

Dean came to live with us the year I left for college. He was a great-looking, good-natured nineteen-year-old from Toronto, one of a dozen high-powered hockey players recruited to play for Ned Harkness at Union College.

I only saw Dean when I came home for vacations, and I liked him. He took me to a frat party at Union and introduced me to the other players; we talked hockey; I remember helping him with an English assignment. He had moved into my grandmother's old room at the end of the hallway, next to my parent's bedroom, and he was obviously grateful to be in a house that adored him and was crazy, like a lot of Schenectady was, about this new Union College hockey program.

My father, mother, and sister never missed a game. Within a year, Union was one of the best teams in the East; within two, one of the best teams in the country. And Dean, all 190 pumped pounds of him, was one of their best, most popular players—fast and hot, a lifeguard on ice skates. The girls loved him. And so, it seemed, did my father.

I barely registered that at the time. Partly because I was so immersed in my own college thing, partly, I think, because it was too painful to consider: Here was the powerfully built son my father had always wanted; here was the hugely successful athlete who could win his love. The minute I had moved out—he had brought in his real son, the true son, the handsome son, the strong son, the loveable son. The Blessed son.

Twenty-five years later, this still stings. Less than when I first faced it in therapy, but some. What I wanted, what Dean wanted, what we all want is really simple: we want our father's Blessing.

Son, I know when you look up, there is a world of men out there who seem to be everything you're not—they're smart and you feel dumb, they're strong and you feel weak, they're loved and you feel unlovable. I just want you to know that, first of all, believe it or not, many of those same men are feeling the same way you're feeling. And most importantly, you too are smart, you too are strong, you too are loveable. Try to remember that about other men, and never forget it about yourself.

Gramps

In some Native American sweats, "grandfathers" are brought to the water-pourer from outside. These "grandfathers" are red-hot rocks. One by one, it is their energy that transforms the darkness of the sweat lodge into radiant, sacred, communal space.

I cried the first time, sitting in that darkness, when I heard the words, "Grandfather coming in," and then our response: "Thank you, Grandfather."

I thought of my grandfather. Gramps. My mother's father, Michael Castelli. All five-foot of him, his wisps of white hair, his soft hands full of Wrigley's gum, his unexpectedly Popeye-big biceps. He kept up on the world, patiently turning the pages of *The Schenectady Gazette* each and every day. He was a quiet guy, but there was something unmistakably principled about him. After he died, I learned that he had stood up to the Black Shirts, Mussolini's thugs, in his tiny Italian village.

I wasn't surprised. I had seen him stand up to my six-foot father, something few people attempted. No, he told my father, he thought the boys had done enough raking and leaf bagging for the time being. He had helped my brother and I as, together, we filled up dozens of bags of the never-before-raked woods in our Hillside Dr. backyard. My father just nodded "OK," and we were free!

I remember Gramps was there when I hit my one and only Little League home run. I smacked the ball over the right fielder's head and I was running around the bases like a crazy man. As I headed into third, my grandfather rose from his plastic folding chair and signaled me with his hands to slow down, no need to rush, the outfielder hadn't even reached the ball yet, if I kept going like this I was going to pass the runner in front of me.

So I did, I slowed down.

My father was all faster, faster, faster—more, more, more—it's not enough, it's not enough, it's not enough.

My grandfather told me it was OK to slow down.

Just recently it occurred to me that I might not have survived my father without my grandfather. Without Gramps's solid presence, his quiet love, his soft blessings...

Thank you, Grandfather.

BLESSING OUR SHADOW

Burying Houdini

I

Houdini died, my father said,
because a man punched him
in the gut before he was ready.

"He could move his organs out of the way,
and then tighten his stomach
like nobody's business."

But this man didn't give him the chance.
He hit Houdini with a powerful right.
His insides burst.

My father respected Houdini.
He talked about him with reverence,
like he talked about Ernie Davis

and the pilot who had survived
a Roman Candle in WWII.
So I respected Houdini.

I decided then and there
a hard stomach was a good thing
since you never knew when a man

might hit you and maybe even kill you.
I did sit-ups every night.
I defended myself with niceness,

hoping to defuse a fatal punch.
I pounded my own belly
until the juices inside me groaned.

When my father hit me
because I'd done wrong
he always did it on my butt.

I could take that.
Somehow it even made my stomach tougher,
especially once the tears set like cement.

But one day, what if my father hit me
like that man hit Houdini,
before I was ready,

before I had done a million sit-ups,
before I could move my heart,
before I had a chance to harden like him?

II
He already had.
A thousand times.
Neither one of us knew it.

III
My father never saw the punch coming.
For 63 years, he had his eyes peeled
for some strange man

to step out of the shadows
and sucker punch his life away:
Dead from an external blow.

Meanwhile, his own body
slowly, finally turned against him:
Dead from fear,

dead from unheeded pain,
dead from a lifetime
of tiny, internal hemorrhaging.

IV

Only since his death
have I begun to learn it's safe
to let my breath all the way out

to soften my belly like a baby's,
and then say to men, and to the world,
go ahead, give me your best shot,

I'm ready now.

Men and Our Shadow

All the gook and gold inside of us. All the parts of us that we have denied, repressed, hidden. All of our unlived life. All our heroes and all our enemies. All the terrors and treasures socked and stocked and locked away. All this is our Shadow.

Robert Bly says a man spends the first twenty years of his life deciding what parts of himself to stick deep in a shadow bag—and the rest of his life trying to get them out again.

Here's some of what I stuffed in my bag as a boy:

1. I stuffed my anger.

2. I stuffed my power.

3. I stuffed my Little Boy.

4. I stuffed my singing.

5. I stuffed my dancing.

6. I stuffed my drawing.

7. I stuffed taking care of myself.

8. I stuffed my penis and my thinness.

9. I stuffed $.

10. I stuffed my spirituality.

Why does a boy do all this stuffing?

Because a boy wants and needs to win his parents' love. And to win this love, the love he needs to survive, he constructs a set of behaviors and attitudes—a persona, a personality—acceptable to his parents. Whatever they bless, he adopts; whatever they curse, or don't acknowledge, he stuffs in the bag.

My own best shot for love and survival was to be the *Good Son*. Anything that didn't fit their idea of *Good Son*…got stuffed into the bag: *A Good Son doesn't get angry*—so my anger got shoved into the bag. *A Good Son is completely unselfish*—so part of my power, part of my sexuality, a big piece of my instinct to take care of myself, all of that got stuffed into the bag.

Now, it's not only our parents that stimulate our stuffing. I had a third-grade music teacher who told me I couldn't carry a tune—my singing slipped into the bag for thirty-five years. You might have had a boy on the playground who told you you threw like a girl; or your brother or a nun who you thought laughed at your lopsided, first-grade drawing; or you froze up when speaking at your friend's birthday party. It's a safe bet you haven't forgotten that—that you stuffed "sports" or "drawing" or "public speaking" deep into the bag. And anytime, for decades after, we have to sing a song, throw a ball, draw a picture, speak to a group...we feel instant shame seep up from the depths of our body and bathe us in embarrassment.

But I want to suggest that for many boys, our fathers are often the foremost dictators of what is, or isn't, in our shadow bags. More than anything, we crave our father's Blessing: we want him to tell us we have all it takes to be a man someday. So, to whatever extent he is present in our life, we watch him for every clue, every hint, every sign of what it is to be a man: a man is big with a deep voice, a man works like a dog or doesn't work at all, drinks beer or drinks milk or drinks both; a man washes his car or his paint brushes on Saturdays, and watches football or "Meet the Press" or Billy Graham on Sundays; a man cooks or doesn't cook, cries or doesn't cry, yells or doesn't yell, sings or doesn't sing, hugs or doesn't hug. And we boys are constant sorters: whatever we see our fathers do or like or are, we adopt; whatever we see our fathers don't do or don't like or aren't, we stuff in the bag.

Or, if we have a horribly abusive father or have been abandoned by our father, we may do the opposite: we may stick everything that is "father"—anger, sexuality, irresponsibility—into our shadow bag.

Probably, most sons do a bit of both: whatever it is about our fathers we can incorporate into our own personality, we do; whatever is too overwhelming about our fathers, too much for us—in my case, for example, my father's anger—we stuff in the bag.

Do you see what's going on here? Our father, "good" or "bad," has his own shadow bag, and we're taking it on, item by item. How could we not be dragging around shadow bags at least as big as our father's bag (who has been dragging around *his* father's bag)? And this is happening not because we or our fathers did anything "wrong"; this process of personality formation-shadow creation happens in the most stable and the most dysfunctional of families. It is an inevitable process of a boy trying to sort out his world in the best way he can—in a way that will enable him to survive and, hopefully, win The Blessing of his father.

And there is an equally inevitable process, usually somewhere in a man's late-thirties or early-forties, when the persona begins to break down and the shadow begins to beckon: a man's so-called mid-life crisis.

What is *not* inevitable is a man's response to such a crisis. A man basically has two choices at this point: (1) he can continue to clutch his mask for dear life and sit on his shadow bag; or (2) he can open the bag and begin to relate to whatever he finds inside.

If we want to be whole men, we have to open this bag. And that takes courage, maybe more courage than anything we have ever attempted in our lives.

I remember opening a lawn bag that had had discarded food scraps sealed in it for a couple of hot summer weeks—meat, vegetables, milk. The maggoty stench that erupted when I untwisted the bag literally knocked me back two steps and made me dry heave.

That's what we expect to get hit with when we open our long-sealed shadow bags—the most god-awful, putrid, rotten "shit" in the entire universe. We are deathly afraid of this, are *sure* of it, in fact: there is nothing more gross, anywhere, than what's in MY bag! It *feels* like garbage because, by our long-ago sorting, it *was* garbage. All the "bad" stuff, gross stuff, shame-contaminated stuff *got* stuffed.

And, truth be told, some of the stuff in there is unsettlingly decomposed. The anger and sadness we stuffed in there three decades ago may have metastasized to rage; an uncomfortableness with our body may now manifest, years later, as revulsion of our body; what once was a tiny fear may now be a full-blown, incapacitating terror. Yes, there is a lot of gook in there that is badly in need of air; and surely, since shadow energy is stronger than the tightest grip, some of those toxins have been leaking out sideways for a while.

And yet Karl Jung, the depth psychologist who coined "shadow" and was one of the shadow's greatest explorers, proposed that perhaps as much as 90% of our shadow is not garbage, but GOLD. All our hidden talents and imprisoned energies are there to be tapped, our wholeness to be won…if we have the courage.

I'm not calling for perfect parents, perfect fathers, so we can have perfect, shadow-less kids. Perfect parents, perfect fathers, and shadowless kids do not exist. But I am suggesting that a father's Blessing can minimize the size of his son's shadow bag. And insofar as a father is courageous enough to open, examine, and embrace the contents of his own bag, he also, necessarily, passes on less baggage to his son.

Let me end with two Blessings, one for the young son, one for the mid-life man.

Son, I see you watching me closely for what it is to be a man. Let me tell you what a man is: A man is strong and loving. And I will do my best to model that strength and love for you. But know you already have that strength and love in you; you already have all it takes—the body, the brain, the heart—to be a strong, loving man. And at a certain point in your life, you will have the strength and love to see and embrace even some of the "ugly" things you can't bear to look at now. You are 360 degrees of radiance. You are a beautiful boy who will grow up to be a beautiful, whole man.

Son, you have been a Good Son long enough. Now it is time for you to be a Whole Man. I bless your courage in opening up your shadow bag and doing your best to embrace what you discover there: I, too, honor your anger; I, too, honor your power; I, too, honor your sexuality and your body; I, too, honor all your re-discovered talents and creativity. I say to you now what I could not say to you when you were a boy: You are beautiful, loving, powerful. You are 360 degrees of radiance. You are whole, you are enough, you are a man.

My Mid-life Crisis

My midlife crisis lasted about a quarter of my life—from roughly 33 to 44. A tough stretch, those eleven years. The wheels never completely came off, but the vehicle that was my life drifted, stalled, flattened, reversed, rutted, rusted, shook, rattled and smoked…My calling stopped calling, my persona got played out, my spirit left town, and my shadow reared up.

I was lost. What had worked, wasn't working. At least not for me. I was still playing the role of the ever-dutiful Nice Guy, the pleasing perfectionist Rescuer, but I was no longer getting much satisfaction from it. Many days, I didn't want to help—I wanted to yell. I wanted to pull hair and howl, "Heal yourself, god damn it!" I wanted out.

Successful in the eyes of the world, I was, in reality, stuck in the limbo between boyhood and manhood. Disconnected: From myself—from my emotions, from my body, from my mission, from my spirit—and from men, especially from my father and from father energy.

And what's a disconnected man-boy to do, especially one who was so severely out-of-touch that he wasn't entirely aware of the depths of his subterranean sadness and shame?

I did what I had been doing all my life when the pain came: I read a fuck-load of books. This time around, though, I was more and more aware that if I slowed down, suspended my reading-frenzy, and listened, one book led to the next—from Bly's *Iron John* to Jung's *Memories, Dreams, Reflections* to Robert Johnson's *Inner Work* to James Hollis' *Tracking the Gods*; from Guy Corneau's *Absent Fathers, Lost Sons* to Moore and Gillette's *King Warrior Magician Lover* to Frank Pittman's *Man Enough*; from Marie-Louise von Franz's *The Way of the Dream* to Marc Ian Barasch's *Healing Dreams* to Greg Levov's *Callings*; from Zweig and Abrams' *Meeting the Shadow* to Bly's *A Little Book on the Human Shadow* to Debbie Ford's *The Dark Side of the Light Chasers*; from Judith Harris' *Jung and Yoga* to Caroline Sutherland's *The Body "Knows"* to Jesse Lynn Hanley's *Tired of Being Tired*; from Julia Cameron's *The Artist's Way* to James Redfield's *Celestine Prophecy* to Neal Donald Walsch's *Conversations with God*; from Grace & Jimmy Boggs' *Conversations in Maine* to Michael Lerner's *Spirit Matters*; from

Judith Orloff's *Intuitive Healing* to Caroline Myss's *Sacred Contracts* to Shakti Gawain's *Living in the Light;* from Jack Kornfield's *A Path with Heart* to Gerri Larkin's *The Still Point Dhammapada* to Pema Chodron's *When Things Fall Apart…*

Jung's idea of synchronicity—there are no accidents—seemed to be playing itself out, however hidden, however slowly, not only in my reading, but in my life at large. Suffering from political withdrawal, I called up Grace Lee Boggs and she invited me for coffee; four years later, through Grace's Detroit Summer, I met the woman who would become my wife. Midway through my mid-life crisis, my father died. His illness and death quickened my desire to understand who we were, this father and son, and what that meant for my own manhood and my fear of fatherhood. Several years later—years full of more reading on men's lives, therapy, personal writing—I bumped into a quiet guy at a party who told me about the Mankind Project's New Warrior Weekend. I knew the second I heard him mention it that the Weekend would be a huge step toward my re-connection.

Over the years, I began to trust that if I had ears to hear, the Universe was speaking to me all the time—through my dreams, through my poems, through my cat and my wife, through the aches and pains in my body. I wasn't some disconnected man-boy with a head full of ideas and an empty gut. I was slowly becoming a man connected to a new home in Detroit, to a loving wife, to a handful of beautiful old friends, to a community of warrior men, to a mother, a sister, a brother. And to a father.

Son, I'm sad to see how much you suffered in your middle years. It pains me tremendously that my not giving you The Blessing earlier in your life is surely one of the reasons for your later suffering. I will say to you now what I was unable to say to you then: You are a strong, loving man, and your strength and your love connects you to this world—to other strong, loving men and women, to rich traditions, to deep truths, to oceans and mountains, to blue whales and black crows.

Black Men

I've watched black men all my life.

I can still see Jim Brown sweeping to his right on a snow-covered Cleveland field, 1965. Willie Mays was my man; Gale Sayers was magic; Muhammad Ali, with his beautiful brashness, completely won my heart. In the world of entertainment, my father, also a watcher of black men, passed on his awe of Sammy Davis Jr.'s acrobatic tap dancing and Nat King Cole's supremely silky voice. Later, much later, there was Malcolm X and James Baldwin, Michael Jordan and Tiger Woods.

In high school, Brendan and I journeyed from our all-white suburb down to the Schenectady Boy's club. We ran up and down the court with young black men, and though I played hard, concentrated on my game, all the while I was watching too. Who were these guys who jumped so high, rapped before rap officially existed, and laughed so easily? My stiff self wanted to be them, to move through the world with their loose grace...

And their big dicks. They had them, I was as sure of that as I was sure of the extra-something they had in their legs to spring them rimward. And I even imagined their extra-long cocks were the source of it all—their cool confidence, their quick anger, even their jumping.

Black men appeared often in my dreams. Most of the time, they were stereotypically scary or violent—looming outside of my house, raping my girl friend. But there was also a well-dressed white-haired black man walking with lonely indifference past me in a parking lot; and a black doctor who invited me into his apartment when I was being chased by evil men.

As an Unblessed son, I have long struggled with the inadequacies of my own body, and out of this personal sense of lacking, I have projected some of my sexual power, my manly confidence, and my physical grace onto the black men I have been watching much of my life. I recognize that my projections here are problematic, to say the least, and, by virtue of their being projections, not necessarily true about black men—but absolutely true *about me*. When a father doesn't tell a son he is enough, that son may turn outward and glorify a group of men whom he believes have what he lacks—or hate them for their alleged superiority.

In this way, racism, like homophobia, may well arise from the fear Unblessed men have that they are not enough.

Son, black or white, you are enough. Right now, just as you are. Your cock is big enough and your body fluid enough. You will be a beautiful, graceful, powerful man in a world of beautiful, graceful, powerful men.

Cops & Doctors

I don't like cops, and I don't like doctors. They both make me mad. Instantly.

Whenever I get instantly mad, I've learned it's not about "Them," whoever "Them" is; it's about me...

So what is it about *me* that hates cops & doctors?

A cop's job is to bust people who do wrong. I don't need anybody to tell me Right/Wrong; I had Right/Wrong beaten into me when I was a wee boy. I've internalized all that. I'm my own cop, and often, I'm an asshole to myself. I beat myself up. When it comes to me, I'm Rodney King *and* a bunch of cops with nightsticks.

A doctor's job is to fix people who are sick. I don't need anybody else to try to fix me; I've been trying to fix me since I was ten years old. I'm broken inside. I'm my own doctor, and often, I violate the Hippocratic oath and first do harm to myself. I'm a doctor with an incurable disease.

Bottom line, when I see a cop or a doctor, I'm suddenly a boy reacting to his father.

Bottom line, I've taken on my father's roles: I am the arbiter of Right and Wrong; I am the fixer of broken things.

Bottom line, I don't want to play cop or doctor anymore—I don't want to bust, I don't want to fix. I want to relax, I want to heal.

Bottom line, I want to bless the crazy cop inside who writes me up; I want to bless the wounded doctor inside who stitches me up.

Inner Cop & Inner Doctor, thank you for the admirable service you've both performed. You did what you thought best to keep me safe and healthy. As a boy, you judged my father would kill me if I did Wrong, so you watched 24/7 to make sure I did all Right; you knew I was deeply hurt, so you offered me what medicine you could to make me better. But I'm no longer a boy. I'm a strong, loving, healing man. You can stop now, rest. Retire to Honolulu, if you want. You've earned it.

Big Guys, Big Stories

I like to hang out with big guys. Large-ass working-class guys who've done some of the macho jobs my skinny, middle-class self has never done. Guys built big who talk big. Truck drivers. Autoworkers. Roofers. Soldiers. Guys who rip shit down and build shit up.... I'm drawn to guys like this, crave their stories. Crave their acceptance.

Last night at a Christmas party I talked to a big guy who fought forest fires in southern California for thirty-one years. He told me there are three things that feed a fire—oxygen, heat, and fuel—and the only one you can do much about is fuel—"You pick a spot. Here. On this side of the road. And you might have to lose 100 houses to save 500." He told me you can get caught between two fires—it happened to him once, and he and his unit had to dig a hole and push their faces into the cool dirt, ride it out. He said how absolutely incredible it was to see 20- or 30,000 acres go up "Just like that"; how beautiful it was at night to watch a fire burn across a mountain or spread from the tops of trees. The more he talked, the more he leaned forward on the couch, his glass of bourbon forgotten, fire in his eyes.

"I told my first wife," he said, "I want to be clear about something: given the choice between forest fires and us, forest fires win. Every time." Their wedding was scheduled for June. "I told her, honey, June's the start of the fire season. I want to be *real, real* clear about something—given the choice between a forest fire and our wedding, the forest fire's gonna win."

No forest fire on their wedding day, but two days later, in the middle of their honeymoon, one jumped off. Then he told me something I already knew: "The forest fire won," he said.

I asked him what was it about fighting a forest fire that made it "better than sex, better than anything I know of," even though I already knew that answer too. "Adrenaline," he said. "It's a rush. You and your men against this thing, this awesome thing that can take you down like that."

I'm a sucker for adrenaline-riddled stories, passionate men who do big things in the company of other passionate men. I've had a fire in my own belly to find a forest fire of some kind or another to fight for the rest of my life. And I don't know how much of that desire is actually hard-wired into us men. Maybe a good chunk of it.

But I know that at least some of this superman urge—this urge to be a big man doing big things—arises because I feel so damn small so much of the time. Physically frail, emotionally soft. That's why I work so god damn hard to get big guys like this ex-fire fighter to like me, think of me as one of the guys. "Hey, Pete might be skinny as shit, a god damn pencil-pusher, but he's alright; he can hang."

My father was a big guy, and he could tell a story. What he didn't know, he'd make up on the spot. I was his best audience. I'd ask him about his childhood and hang on every word; he was a private man, but that only meant he had all sorts of long-buried good stuff to share.

I wish he had been a little more interested in listening to my buried stuff. I wish I had been more insistent on telling him—on dropping my spectator's role, and telling him about *my* life for a change. But some deep part of me didn't believe I had any good stories to tell. Stories are what other people told—what big guys told to small boys.

Son, your whole life is a beautiful story. My own story has been made more beautiful, more funny, more loving because you are so much a part of it. Tell your story, show your power, share your love. I'm sorry I wasn't listening more closely then; there is nothing in this world I'd rather be hearing now.

Stan the Man Talks Back

The Blessing—give me a friggin' break! Why don't you just get over it? Just stop already. You're 45, for Christ sake. Enough is enough. OK. I hear you've got a little father issue, but who doesn't?

(That's Stan the Man. Stan the Man is strictly Old School: he's the part of me who thinks I need to be tough, no-nonsense.)

That's my point, Stan. Who doesn't? I don't know a man who doesn't have a father issue; I know very few men who have gotten The Blessing. It's killing us. Nearly *all* of us.

In your judgment, Doc...

Yes, in my judgment what most men are suffering from is an absence of anointment. Not getting the Blessing. Most men are suffering because they never got the Blessing from their father. And by the way, I'm not a doctor; I have a Master's Degree. In English.

This is getting better by the minute! So you're not even a shrink? You have a degree in reading long boring books, and I'm suppose to take you seriously?

You don't have to take me seriously. You shouldn't take me seriously. Hey, if what I'm saying doesn't resonate with anything you've felt or experienced—if your life is working for you, if things between you and your father are cool, if you don't feel like there's some hole in your life that you've been trying to fill up in all sorts of addictive ways—you don't need what I'm saying. You've already got The Blessing. I'm happy for you. All I can say is I've been a son all my life—that's my biggest credential—and I've been trying to figure out what I need to fill the hole once and for all. To feel whole. To feel like I'm enough.

All right, all right. Since I'm a little bored today and I feel like messin' with you, I'll keep talking.... So we never got this Blessing. Big deal. How would it help, really?

How would it help? It would help because it's the reason why we men are constantly trying to prove ourselves. I'm constantly measuring myself against other men—Am I man enough? When I go into a car shop—am I man enough? When I shake hands with a man—am I man enough? When I look at my bank account, my body, my life—am I man enough?

That's you. You have this messed-up "I'm too small" thing. You're afraid to be Big, man! I've been telling you for years to lift weights.

I know you have. But I'm talking about INNER strength. I see guys who are Hulks on the outside, but I still feel their inner fear and shame.

So you have the answer, do you, for all men? This Blessing that we were also suppose to have missed?

I believe it explains a lot of our behavior, yes.

Great. So what the hell are we all suppose to do about it now, Doc? You're just stirring things up. Whatever happened, or didn't happen—that was frickin' years ago. Personally, I want to get on with my life.

I want to get on with my life too, Stan. But we're stuck, most men are stuck. In our boyhood. If we didn't get The Blessing, most likely that's the stage we're stuck in: always having to prove ourselves; not thinking we're enough; trying to fill up our father-hole with all sorts of addictions.

You didn't answer my damn question. What the hell are we supposed to do about it now?

First, we need to admit that our lives are not working for us; that we're stuck.

Fuck "stuck"! You know what? You're soft, Doc. Bottom line, you're soft. You need to toughen up, that's what you need.

That's what my father believed, and so did many of my coaches—and so does the military. And possibly, in some situations, with some boys, that might be effective. But for me, the bottom line is Blessing: if my father or stepfather or some strong, loving man recognizes my love and my power, I will feel loving and powerful. I'll then be willing and able to do the "tough" things men are sometimes required to do: to not run when the going gets tough, to stay the course, to hold the fort, no matter what emotions come up.

I don't buy it. I didn't get this Blessing thing, and I don't run. I'm no wimp.

I never said you were a wimp. Part of the Blessing is that the father tells his son it's OK to feel certain things: sadness, fear, anger, even shame. Go ahead and cry, son, go ahead and feel your fear.

Feel your fear? What the hell does that mean?

Just acknowledge it. Or better: have it acknowledged by a man you respect. If he says it's "normal," then I'm not a punk for feeling it.

But you are a punk if you don't do anything about it. If you let fear paralyze you.

OK. I see where you're going with that. I don't know how to answer that, exactly. It may mean we have to "do" something else. We might have to fight; we may even have to run in certain circumstances. But if we have our fathers admit to the fear, it's not then something we have to pretend we don't have, pretend we don't feel.

So we end up growing up to be sissies!

I don't think so. We end up growing up to me men who are in touch with our feelings, including fear and sadness and shame. We end up growing up to be men who are powerful *and* loving.

I'm skeptical as hell.

Well, I'm not 100% myself here.

I thought you had it all worked out.

Some days, that's what it feels like. Then things change.

Shit happens.

Exactly. Fear kicks in, or shame, or sadness, or anger—and I'm not so sure, and I feel like running, and maybe I'll never be that powerful, loving man I want to be.

I got one more question for ya, Doc, and then I gotta split. Unlike some people I know, I got things to do.

Shoot.

This Blessing idea of yours, it seems like you can say it in a sentence? Something like, "Son, you're going to be a kick-ass, loving man, and I'm proud of you," right?

That's right, and I like your way of putting it.

So why do you need a whole damn book then?

You know, originally I never thought this would be a book. But the more I thought about my life and the life of other men, the more I saw how The Blessing was central to so much of our healing. And that there were a hundred different situations to say it in, each one slightly different, and I felt a deep need to give voice to those hundred variations. For myself, as much as for the men, and women, who read the book.

A hundred ways, is that what I heard you say, Doc? Take it from Stan the Man, that's gonna be one boring-ass book.

We'll see…Stan, before you go, I want to tell you I'm glad you're one of my voices, one of my energies, one of the parts of me.

Don't bullshit me, Doc. You want me dead.

Sometimes. On my pissed-off bad days, I wish I could just go in and surgically remove you—cut you out, and be done, once and for all. Cut out the hard-ass voice of my father and those coaches and John Wayne—all those Old Warriors—

Is that who I am, an Old Warrior?

Yes. You're my internalized Old Warrior. Tough, gritty, no-nonsense…

Keep going. I'm enjoying this.

Aloof, lonely…

Hey, hey, enough. You don't have to go there…

To lonely? Are you lonely, Stan?

I told you, enough. End of conversation.

Fair enough. Can we talk again some time?

I'll just kick your ass again.

I look forward to that ass kicking.

Me too, Doc.

Bullies

In elementary school, I was a skinny, crew cut kid who hauled around a library of books in his father's big old brown briefcase. I should have been prime bully-meat, a bully's dream. I was all but begging some big jerk sixth-grader to rip the briefcase out of my hand, shake the books all over the ground, and then crown me in leather.

It never happened. Maybe because I was also a good, little athlete who starred in gym class. Maybe because I had already read Dale Carnegie's *How To Win Friends and Influence People*, and knew how to make even the baddest bully feel better about himself. Maybe I was just so supremely, pathetically innocent I was invisible to bully radar. Maybe bullies sensed I had enough bullying going on at home and cut me some slack. Maybe I was just lucky.

In any case, I've spent most of my life trying my damnedest not to be a bully—and being enraged at people who I judged were bullies. I think I've done pretty well with the first part, but I've acted like a tyrant myself when it comes to people I perceive as bullies. I've hated parents who appeared to be bullying their kids and teachers who seemed to bully their students; I've detested the Bobby Knights who I judged bullied their players, and presidents who I judged bullied militarily weaker countries and poorer people. In a supermarket, on the TV, if I spy a bully, my blood pressure crescendos and I want to lace my fingers around his (sometimes her) neck and squeeze until the bastard is dead. This, I judge, is not always an emotionally healthy, spiritually mature reaction on my part.

Lately, for my own good, I've been trying to understand bullying a little better.

My wife tells me that in her middle school, there is not so much a couple of bullies as a *chain* of bullies. A bully pecking order where each bullied kid finds a lesser kid to bully, right on down the line.

This makes me sad, but it feels true. My hunch is bullying comes out of not feeling like you're enough, that you're small, that you're ugly—and you're going to make yourself feel a little bigger by beating the beauty out of somebody else. And who doesn't feel like they're not enough, that they're not mirror-mirror-on-the-wall ugly when they're an adolescent in middle school?

Especially if you're a boy, like most boys, who didn't get The Blessing.

I didn't get The Blessing as a boy, and I was bullied by my father, both corporally and emotionally. He truly believed the hitting was "discipline," a father's duty, and without it, his sons' lives would go astray in some terrible way; and he also was major-league disconnected from his own childhood feelings of sadness and smallness. Which doesn't mean he didn't bully my brother and me—he did, and it hurt—but it also means he was an Unblessed, bullied boy himself doing his best to be a father. And when *I* want to get in the face of Bully Bobby or Bully Georgie, that's the Unblessed, bullied boy in me projecting a son's anger onto virtual strangers—reacting like the bully I never want to be.

The Blessing is the best immunization to bullying.

Son, you are strong, loving and loveable. Beautiful. People might mock your strength, ridicule your love, attack your beauty. Understand where their bullying is coming from—it has little to do with you, and much to do with them. They're feeling their own weakness, unlovableness, ugliness. Remember that. And remember you have all you need to be a strong, loving, beautiful man. A man who, at some point, is even strong enough, loving enough, and beautiful enough to forgive those who feel and act like they're not enough.

George Bush & Me

I didn't vote for George W. Bush. I think his policies are harmful to American and harmful to the world. But we have a lot in common, and I think I understand him.

He comes from a privileged world; I come from a privileged world. He appears to have an addiction to absolutes; I, too, have an addiction to absolutes. Most significantly, I judge he's a son trying to please a powerful father; and I am a son who tried to please a powerful father.

In short, from what I can see, George W. Bush is a scared, uncertain boy doing his absolute best to appear like a man. I can say this because, at 45, I am just now stepping out of my own timid boyhood into some semblance of manhood. On my New Warrior Training Adventure weekend four years ago, there were twenty-three such boy-men; the current President of the United States is just one of the hundreds I've met since. As far as I can tell, Bush, as well as Gore and Clinton, are all in the same row boat as a lot of men in America: boys, many of us, who hide much of the best of ourselves in order to appear strong in the eyes of other men, especially in the eyes of our Fathers.

In truth, despite my strong political differences, I feel for Bush. I know all too well how hard it is to wake up in your bed feeling like a small, lost son—and walk out the door pretending you're the powerful, certain father. It's been difficult pulling that off in my little world; I can't imagine how hard it must be to maintain that in the face of the *whole* world, as the President must do.

What I wish for George W. Bush is what I wish for all men, myself included. I wish some strong, loving man would grab him by the shoulders, look him in the eye, and tell him he can stop pretending. Tell him he's man enough. Tell him he's got nothing to prove—to himself, to his father, to other men, to the world. And then show him how it's possible for a powerful man to love powerfully—not with guns and Us/Them rhetoric, which are the weapons of scared boys, but as King loved, as Gandhi loved: with a big, courageous heart and a clear, deep sense of how we are all connected in this world.

Forgive Me, I Knew Not What I Was Doing

A boy arrives in this world swathed in beauty. If the people around him, particularly his father, mirror that in-born beauty, acknowledge it, affirm it, that boy will grow into a man who can look in the mirror and see the beauty for himself.

If, instead, a boy is terrorized by his father, things get ugly in a hurry. Rather than knowing and feeling his own inherent beauty, this boy only knows the ugliness mirrored by his father. The terror—physical, emotional, sexual—has overwhelmed beauty. So when the terrorized boy looks into the mirror…he can only see and feel his own emptiness and ugliness.

I don't know a worse crime than robbing a boy of his beauty.

I don't think most fathers mean to do it. I don't think my father meant to do it to me. They just do unto others what was done unto them. Someone, most likely *their* father, scared the beauty out of them. When it comes to their sons, the festering ugliness wins out. Instead of The Blessing, these fathers pass on The Curse.

Something tells me, though, it's never too late for a father to own what he did and ask his son for forgiveness. I'm not saying it's guaranteed; I'm not saying there won't be tears and anger, and who knows what else; I'm not saying it will be instantaneous. I'm just saying that, in most cases, the beauty is still down there deep in us, somehow intact, but we sons often can't see it until our fathers come clean and tell us. To ask our forgiveness, then to Bless us, transforms the terror and the ugliness into love and beauty.

Son, I'm so sorry for what I did to you. Please, please forgive me. When I think of it now, it hurts me more deeply than anything I've ever done in my life. It hurts so badly because what it tells you about you is a lie. An absolute lie. This is the truth: you are a beautiful, wonderful man. From the moment I first held you, I could feel that truth in my arms and see it in your eyes: you were a beautiful, wonderful, strong, intelligent boy and you have grown up to be a beautiful, wonderful, strong, intelligent man. Forget everything else. Everything else is a lie. Remember this truth.

The Father of All Projects

I'm not happy unless I'm consumed by a Project. The bigger the better. I want something I can lose myself in. I want something that is bigger than myself. I want to *Do* something that will change a lot of lives for the better. I was a revolutionary communist for eight years trying to change the whole world. Now that's my kind of Project.

Some of this is healthy. Some of this is a man's sense of Mission; of making meaning out of his life.

Some of this, maybe a lot of it for me, is unhealthy. My reasoning is all messed up: I'm only worth something if I'm doing something to help others. I need to earn my existence on this earth, which means my existence is conditional. In short, I'm worthless…unless I have a Project.

My wife asked me the other day, "Are you happier when you have a Project?"

"Hell yes!"

"Because you feel better about yourself?"

"Hell yes!"

"Let me ask it another way: Are you more content?"

Ouch. That slowed me down. "More content? Well, I wouldn't say more content."

"I guess that's what I mean when I say "happier"—more content."

My wife is good at asking good questions. She knows me. She knows as well as I do the source of my Project-mania.

My Project-mania comes from my father, my father-wound, my father-hole. My father always had a Project: golf (club champion), flying (across the Atlantic in a tiny Cessna), skeet shooting (All-American). And clearly, he was extremely successful in his Projects. I watched his incessant effort, his relentless discipline, his fierce focus, his ceaseless self-flagellation.

Ah, I said, this is what men do! Good men, anyway, like my father. They pick out some worthy Project and they throw themselves into it, head, heart, and soul. I can do that!

And I did.

Until dozens of noble projects and forty years later, I was burned-out. And still not feeling like a man.

My father never took on the project of fatherhood. I'm learning to forgive him for that. His was John Wayne's generation, and my father, for all his tremendous accomplishments and seeming invincibility, was a deeply wounded man. An Unblessed man who did his best. And his best, what he passed on to me in lieu of The Blessing, was a passion for Projects.

A father-wound always has some compensation. In my case, a passion for Projects isn't always a negative thing. Writing this book on The Blessing has been a Project—a project in line with my present Mission of Blessing Unblessed sons. And I have found some contentment, and forgiveness, in writing it.

Truth Junkie

Truth is, I'm a capital "T" Truth addict—a junkie who has searched all his life to mainline the purest Truth straight to his soul.

I started young—Norman Vincent Peale's *The Power of Positive Thinking* when I was ten. Then it was on to Dale Carnegie's *How To Stop Worrying and Start Living*, Maxwell Maltz's *Psycho-Cybernetics*, Thomas a Kempis' *Imitation of Christ*. All those and many more before high school, and right through high school.

In college, it was beautiful Camus and the existentialists; in grad school, brilliant Marx and the communists.

Later, I had an intense affair with Stephen Covey's *Seven Habits of Highly Successful People*. After that, I shifted into a softer, feminine self-help cycle—Judith Orloff's *Intuitive Healing* and Caroline Myss' *Sacred Contracts*.—along with all-things Jungian. Most recently, I've dived deep into the Buddhist world of Pema Chodron, and then surfaced with Byron Katie.

I'm not right, and god damn it, these books were going to make me right. A silver sentence somewhere that would clean me out and fill me up. I read with a pen in my hand and the sound of boulders falling in an hourglass: Not enough time, not enough time, not enough time. Not enough time to fix all my fault lines, drain the swamp, re-paint my soul, and save the world.

My name is Peter, and I'm addicted to Truth.

The good news about my addiction is I don't have the time or the taste for petty addictions like alcohol and drugs, sex, food, work. There is no room in my tight little perfectionist universe for excessive consumption of beer or porn or Jolly Ranchers; I am frying bigger fish.

The bad news is my search for Big "T" Truth knows no rest. With the clock right there in your head ticking like a motherfucker, how can you rest for even one milli-second if you believe the fate of your soul and the fate of the world depend on your efforts?

Needless to say, I don't sleep all that well.

How did this start, this relentless, desperate search for the Truth? How did I get so fucked-up?

The simple truth is, I didn't get The Blessing. The Blessing is like an inoculation for a whole lot of excessive behavior, including, I suspect, my Truth hunt.

Son, I love the way you want to try to understand yourself and the world. Go for it, dive right in and explore. There are worlds of truths out there and in you to discover and re-discover. And know, too, that this is one of those truths: You are bright and beautiful even before you open that book and begin searching. You have all it takes, all you need to be a strong, loving, truth-seeking man.

The Rescuer Par Excellance

Boys who are terrorized when they're young could go one of two ways. If they unconsciously throw all that terror and anger back at the world, they become bullies. If they unconsciously decide nobody should ever have to experience all that terror and anger, they become rescuers.

I'm really not sure how it works out, how one boy becomes a bully, one becomes a rescuer. It might have to do with the intensity and/or timing of the terrorizing; or sibling order; or genes—or a prickly mixture of all of these. But I'm reasonably sure they are two sides of the same co-dependent coin: the bully creates victims for the rescuer to rescue.

In any case, I became a rescuer. And not just any garden-variety rescuer—but a Rescuer Par Excellance. In a sense, it's been my calling, my mission. My addiction.

Old people needed to be rescued from their loneliness; young kids needed to be rescued from their shame; women needed to be rescued from their poor self-image; sick people needed to be rescued from their illness; poor people needed to be rescued from their poverty…And I was just the man to do it. All of it.

The first woman I "fell in love with"—a beautiful, intelligent woman—I fell in love with precisely because she didn't realize she was a beautiful, intelligent woman. It became my mission to rescue her from her pathetic misconception.

Many years later, I attempted to rescue another beautiful, intelligent woman who also had the advantage (from a rescuer's perspective) of being older, poor, black, and in end-stage renal failure. This rescue attempt—following as it did the failure of my greatest rescue mission of all as a revolutionary trying to save the entire world, and coinciding with my long-standing rescuing stance toward my disadvantaged community college students—broke me. I was on empty, emotionally burned out, depressed. I got pneumonia. I was literally forced, for the first time in my life, to abort my rescuing of others and to rescue myself.

And for the first time in my life, I began to understand that the person I had been trying to rescue all those years in all those guises…was myself. *I* was a beautiful, intelligent human being. I had projected those buried parts of myself, this gold, onto women, the working-class, my students. I had spent much of my life's energy excavating these precious, priceless qualities in others, but I couldn't see that beautiful gold in myself.

Son, thank you for seeing the gold in other people, especially when they couldn't see that gold in themselves. And my wish for you is to see your own gold—your own beauty, your own intelligence. I see it. I see you have all you will ever need to be a strong, loving man.

Swing Low, Sweet Chariot

"When scientists block testosterone in male baby songbirds, they never sing. But they also never sing if, at a precise time in their childhood, they don't hear their relatives singing. So the cause of the singing is this: A male baby hears a song, which starts a process that uses testosterone to build his brain in such a way that he sings."

—Ann Finkbeiner, in a *New York Times* book review of "Sex On The Brain"

A friend of mine had been dating a woman for about six intense months. One day she asked him, "There's something I'd like you to do for me. Would you do it?"

That's a dangerous question for men, especially when coming from a woman. But my friend is no coward; he had recently made a habit of pushing through all kinds of fear. "I'm not sure what you're going to ask, but I think I can do it," he told her. And as he told me, "I was ready for anything—quit your job? I could handle that. Marry me? Maybe even that."

She was a wise woman. She had seen my friend be smart, successful, funny, kind—what she wanted to see was my friend being vulnerable.

"Would you sing to me?" she asked.

"Damn it," he told me, "anything but *that*! I hadn't sung a note in twenty years. To anyone. Not even in the shower. I was terrified. I wanted to renegotiate."

He did it, though. A Billy Joel song. "At first, nothing came out. Just cracking and creaking. Then it got a little better. I still sounded like shit, but she loved it."

We just went to their wedding.

My dad sang quite a bit. He had a deep, rich bass that he'd sing with Nat King Cole or Sinatra or tender Elvis. My voice didn't sound like his. How the heck did he get so low? I felt ashamed of my squeaky, weak notes.

And then Mr. Dowler, my fourth-grade music teacher, shut me up for years. We were having auditions for the school choir. I was the last to try-out. I got a couple of lines into "America, The Beautiful" when he told me to stop. "You can't carry a tune," he told me. "Sorry."

I've heard a dozen men tell similar stories. Sometime early, someone told them they couldn't sing. And so they didn't. If there's one thing a boy will avoid at all costs, it's shame.

I was at a Warrior-Monk retreat last summer, sitting around a campfire. Everybody else had gone to bed. In fact, I had headed that way myself, then turned around and went back to the fire.

"Glenn," I asked, "can you teach me to sing?"

Glen had been singing all night, competently, joyfully. "No problem," he said.

"How the hell do you do it?"

"You just open your mouth. You just start singing. It's inside of you somewhere. It's just blocked for the moment, that's all."

We sang "Swing Low, Sweet Chariot." My voice has grown deep like my father's, and "Swing Low" is one of the few songs that didn't sound all-out hideous when I attempted it. Glenn, more of a tenor, had to reach down for this one, but he didn't mind. We sang together. It sounded pretty good, except I still wasn't hitting some of the lowest notes.

"Don't worry about the notes," he said. "I like to get a picture in my head of my ideal audience, who I'm singing to or what I'm singing for. If I get that, the notes will take care of themselves."

I nodded. I knew this was true for writing, I had experienced it—but singing was a whole different can of worms. I was suspicious.

"This is originally a slave song," Glenn went on. "Imagine you're a slave. An old man in the middle of a huge field. You've been pickin' cotton your whole life. Seems like ten lives. You're tired. You're dead tired. You want to go home…And you look up and see these angels coming to take you there, to just sweep you off your feet and take you there. You're suddenly filled with joy. For me, this isn't a sad song, it's a joyful one. A song of liberation. Try it that way and see how it feels."

I did, and I damn near cried. Tears of joy. Joy for the old slave going home, joy for my liberated voice.

Like those male songbirds in the quote above, we men are built to sing. All we need is someone to inspire our vulnerability like my friend's wife, someone to model singing like Glenn, someone to Bless our voice and to turn us loose.

Loving What Is

Is it possible that my father *did* give me The Blessing? Is it possible that that is just an unexamined thought I have clung to—and that this whole fat book is just another attempt to "prove" I'm right, to preserve my wound? Or put another way: "My father never gave me The Blessing"—story or reality?

Byron Katie would suggest that's a wonderful question, and until I examine the thought "My father never gave me The Blessing," I'll stay a victim. Her book, *Loving What Is*, is the most rigorously honest book I have come across on examining shadow.

Let me run that thought, "My father never gave me The Blessing," through her four-question inquiry and then see if I can own the shadow in what Katie calls "the turnaround."

1. *"Is it true?"* Is it true that my father never gave me The Blessing? It certainly *feels* true, but then again, says Katie, so does any belief we've held tightly to for so many years.

2. *"Can you absolutely know that it's true?"* Can I absolutely know that it's true that my father never gave me The Blessing? Do I know for sure he never told me I had all it takes to be a strong, loving man? Might he have said that to me when I was a baby, a toddler? Might he have whispered it, or something like it—"Petey, I'm proud of you"—as he closed my door each night? Might he have said it to himself or to my mother when I went away to school and he was missing me? Might he have said it in the last several months of his life as he lay dying in intensive care? Might he have said it in a way that I just couldn't hear or wasn't able to hear?

   No, I cannot say with absolute certainty that my father never gave me The Blessing.

3. *"How do I react when I think that thought?"* How do I react when I think the thought, "My father never gave me The Blessing"? Sometimes I get sad, sometimes angry; sometimes I feel shame. I want to cuss my father

out—"Fuck you!" "What was so fucking hard about saying I was OK!"? Or I go aloof, disappear into my room, my head, my books. My stomach works overtime and I sleep like shit at night. I cook up grand Projects that, when completed, will earn The Blessing I think I never got. I see Unblessed sons everywhere; every man has been wounded by his father. And I ask questions of these men to get the dirt on their fathers and thereby "prove" myself right—"See, look at what he did or didn't do, look at all us poor, sonofabitch Unblessed sons…" Finally, I am afraid to have children myself.

4. *"Who would I be without the thought?"* Who would I be without the thought, "My father never gave me The Blessing"? I'd be free—free of the anger, the shame, the sadness. Free of the Projects. Free of the weight of Unblessed sons everywhere I turn. Free to love my father. Free to have my own children.

And now it's time for *"The Turnaround."* Here's where you see if what you have written about others is as true or truer when you apply it to yourself; here is where you point the finger back at yourself and own all you can of what you've projected onto others. "My father didn't give me The Blessing" "turns around" in at least three ways: (a) "My father *did* give me The Blessing; (b) "I didn't give *my father* The Blessing"; (c) "I didn't give *myself* The Blessing." Since this is the crux of the shadow work, I will take the time to look at each of these turnarounds.

    a. "My father did give me The Blessing"—true or truer? I know he blessed me in a number of ways (I write about those later)—and could it be that all of those blessings add up to The Blessing? Maybe.

    b. "I didn't give my father The Blessing"—in what ways might that be as true or truer than "My father didn't give me The Blessing"? Did I ever tell my father he was a strong, loving man? No, not directly, and not when he was alive—though I often felt it. So, this turnaround is at least as true as the original.

    c. "I didn't give myself The Blessing"—as true or truer? Did I ever tell myself I had all it takes to be a strong, loving man? Occasionally, but not consistently. Instead of blaming my father for not giving me The Blessing, might it be *my* responsibility to find the means and the men to Bless myself? Yes, that feels true.

So after all that inquiry and turn around, where do I stand: did I, or did I not, get The Blessing from my father? Story—or reality?

In all honesty, I would have to say "My father never gave me The Blessing" is the most real story of my life. And because it feels so damn real—and I have so much at stake in holding to that story, including the integrity of this book—I am reluctant to let it go. So the only truthful thing I can do now is to ask Katie's four questions plus the turnaround every time the thought, "My father never gave me The Blessing" arises. In that way, I am learning to love what is—which, finally, is the essence of The Blessing.

BLESSING OUR WOMEN

Elmer Ave.

When I was a boy, we sometimes went to my father's parents' house Sundays after church. This was the same house on Elmer Avenue in Schenectady, NY they had moved into in 1941, the first year of WWII, when my father was seven; the same house that, two years later, held Uncle John's body after he had been killed by friendly fire; the same house that my father's oldest brother left at 17—signed off by his mother, not his father—to go fight in the War. Elmer Avenue was, finally, a place of their own after a hellish Depression where BaPa, my father's father, had lost his job and had had a nervous breakdown, and the three older children had been temporarily sent off to relatives in Syracuse and Detroit, and my father to an orphanage. But some of the Depression's heaviness had moved in with them and was, like the nicotine on the walls, still there thirty years later.

Though it was early afternoon when we arrived, the living room was always thick with shadows. My father sat stiffly in a chair directly across from his mother, while my brother, sister, and I sat at polite attention on the only bit of color in that room, my grandmother's uncompromising red sofa. My mom, though present, disappeared, swallowed up somewhere by shadow. And BaPa disappeared too, behind a newspaper in his chair, or up to his room. The entire living room revolved around this ninety-pound woman grotesquely haloed in damp lamplight, her lips tight around a cigarette, her posture twisted from a hunched back, her abnormally large black eyes floating proudly off in space after her latest acid-tongued observation.

I don't remember my grandmother ever looking at her son; I don't remember them laughing together or hugging. BaPa and my father had brief moments of warmth, especially when they talked about guns and hunting; but it was clear even to me that his father, a physically powerful man who playfully crunched our hands when he shook them, lacked the emotional strength to stand up to his wife's razor-sharp coldness and give his family The Blessing. Elmer Avenue was the only place my father didn't seem to have his usual power; he was more a scared boy of seven than a grown man with a family.

I cherished the few stories I cajoled out of my Dad about his childhood. How he and his brother Pat, both strong-armed athletes, would heave baseballs right over the top of Elmer Ave. Elementary School. How a gang of friends would romp and rough-

house at Vale cemetery three or four blocks away. I think I wanted to see my father playing outside, in the light, away, if only temporarily, from the unforgiving darkness of this house.

When, after fifty years, he finally left Schenectady, my father said it was because of the cold, the snow, the winters. I think he was trying to leave behind the cold and heaviness of that house: the pain of growing up in the middle of a Depression and a World War with a fearful father and a twisted mother.

Disappearing Men

Women, know this about us:
We are disappearing men.

We disappear into beer.
We disappear into pizza & coke
    into politics & art & God.
We disappear into work
    into books
        into porn and Fantasy Football.
We disappear into the past and into the future.
We disappear into our heads and into the woods.
We disappear into anger & sadness, fear & shame.
We disappear into bars, gyms, jails,
    cars, caves, TV sets.
And sometimes, we even disappear into relationships.

There is no place we won't disappear to
    if we think our father will meet us there
    and Bless us—
or no place we won't disappear to
    to forget our father never Blessed us.

Women, know it's not your fault.
Know you can't find us or fix us.
You are not our fathers,
You are not a circle of men.

All you can do is let us go
when we finally decide
to claim The Blessing

and be there with us
when we finally return
to share The Blessing.

Woman-Hunger

I've had days, weeks, months even, when women were more important to me than eating. I chased them, wrote poems about them, dreamed them. Women were the Answer. Women were my Holy Communion. Women would ease the pain, bandage the wound, fill the hole. Give me The Blessing.

We men can be so ravenous when it comes to women that woman-hunger and father-hunger gets all mixed up together.

What is this woman-hunger all about? Two things, I think. Actually, one's the shallow version, one's the deeper version of the same thing: men believe women can make us whole.

(1) *Shallow:* We've been taught that getting women, scoring pussy, is proof of our manhood—proof for ourselves, and for others. If I can win this one beautiful woman…I am a man, and other men will know I am a man. Music videos, TV, and movies offer this as the best and only solution for unhappy men: she's out there somewhere, you just have to find her and win her. Millions of men have tried it, from Adam to Clinton. Maybe we watched our big brother try it. Or our uncle or neighbor or buddy. Or our father.

(2) *Deeper:* Scared of own feminine—our feelings, our Eros, our interconnectedness, our intuition, our beauty—fearful that these wonderful qualities make us less manly, and unschooled in how to integrate them into our own personality, we project them on to women. Then we try to merge with women to acquire the very qualities we gave away.

In short, we believe the Right Woman will complete us: that we are a half-circle…and this woman is the other, matching half-circle…and together, finally, we will be whole. When it doesn't work with this Right Woman—we move on to the next Right Woman, and the next…James Hollis calls it "The Eden Project," this lost Eve/Mother/Magical Other we are forever trying to get back to—this perpetually unfulfilling search to find the *She* who will fill up the hole in our life.

So how do we stop this frantic, fruitless, woman-hungry frenzy?

You're probably not going to like my answer: we men need to do the work to recognize and embrace our own feminine energy—our earthiness, our spirit of connection and relationship, our imagination and intuition. Most of us men are

Logos-centered ("reason," "mind") left-brainers; we need to tap our Eros-driven ("love," "body") right brain. The uncomfortable truth is that before we can have a successful relationship or marriage with a woman, we must develop a successful relationship with the unconscious "woman" within us. If we don't honor and integrate our deep feminine energies, we will almost certainly find ourselves back on the "Right Woman" treadmill to hell.

Our fathers didn't know this. And because they didn't know this, because they hadn't acknowledged, accepted, and integrated their own feminine energies and qualities, they couldn't tell us the truth about women and our manhood.

Our fathers were macho half-men chasing half-woman in order to feel whole or powerful; or they were unhappily married half-men, angry half-men, who felt tricked out of their wholeness or power by the half-woman they had married; or maybe fearful half-men who had married the Warrior energy they couldn't find in themselves. Many of them, I'm sad to say, were misogynistic, homophobic half-men: if you are deeply afraid and hateful of your own femininity, it is impossible for you, finally, to honor and love the femininity in another—in either women or men.

Bottom line, our half-men fathers deeply believed women could give them The Blessing…and women can't. Women can be a huge part of our life, our happiness and our growth, yes, but women cannot give men The Blessing. Women cannot lead us out of the world of our mothers; and marrying a woman in order to acquire the necessary feminine qualities of earthy relatedness, imagination, intuition is a dead-end. This work is men's work, and our own work.

Here is how a whole father, a man who had done some deep shadow work, might Bless women and the femininity of his woman-hungry son.

Son, women are wonderful. Women are beautiful, sensual, connected, and wise. But consuming woman after woman won't make you a man. You already have all you need to be a man. So, relax. Slow down. Honor your own beauty and sensuality and connectedness and wisdom. Love the "woman" in you as strongly as you love the women in the world. In fact, the only way to truly love the women in the world is to love the "woman" in you. That's what strong, loving men do.

Wise Women

I've always known women knew things I didn't know. Important things. I didn't just want to sleep with a woman; I also wanted to find out what she knew that I was clueless about (which included sex).

Beginning with my first girl friend, Lauren, all the way to my wife, Julia, I've been blessed with more than my share of wise women. They've shown me the spirit of art; the power of intuition; the comfort of cycles; the virtue of vulnerability. And rarely, rarely did they shame me with their showing.

I thank them all for all of that.

I also eventually realized that there were certain things these wise women didn't know or couldn't tell me or couldn't convince me of. They were clearly smarter in a multitude of ways from many of the clueless men in my world, but that didn't mean they could replace men for me. Although I usually felt more comfortable and whole in their presence than I did with men; and though they certainly could have hurt me by shaming me—which, again, they rarely did; I never felt these women had the power, I'm sad to say, to heal the deep shame already growing in me long before I lusted after their bodies and their knowledge.

Finally, to heal that primary shame I had to turn back to the world of men.

Like it or not, I had to have men tell me my body was OK, my penis was big enough, my emotions were welcome. A host of strong, loving women have told me I am a strong, loving man, and although I deeply appreciated that, I didn't believe it; I didn't believe it until I was told I was a strong, loving man by other strong, loving men.

I believe this is true for many men. And if it is, women, hear this: You didn't cause your man's primary shame, and you can't heal it. At least not alone. The best you can do—and it's a lot—is to not add to his shame, and to support him when he is ready to connect with other men.

Over the course of my life, I have been blessed with a cadre of wonderful, non-shaming women who have bestowed their wisdom and blessings upon me. But it is only men, ultimately, who can give me The Blessing.

What About My Mother?

This is a book about fathers and sons. About my father and our relationship. What about mothers, my mother? What is the mother's role in The Blessing?

I have always felt blessed by my mother. I have always felt she believed in me—in my intelligence, in my goodness. But I didn't fully trust her blessing. I couldn't help but figure in her incredible bias: I was her son, for Christ sake; of course she's going to think I'm wonderful! Big deal. And sometimes I actually felt hemmed in by her high estimation of me: she thought I was the perfect Good Boy, so I had to *be* the perfect Good Boy. More and more, I felt suffocated and wanted some distance.

So like many men, I was caught between my father's aloofness and my mother's proximity; I had too little father and too much mother. Somehow, I wanted to move from my mother's arms to my father's hug; from being the apple of my mother's eye to the hero of my father's eye. I had a deep, but barely conscious desire to escape from the world of mothers and enter the world of fathers.

But the centripetal pull of the mother's world is immense. Mother is breasts, warmth, comfort—boyhood. Around and around a boy could go, never quite breaking free, always returning to his mother or some woman/wife/lover serving as his surrogate mother. And if his birth mother wasn't warm and comforting, here's a second (or a third, or a fourth, or a...) chance to find a "mother" who is.

To break this cycle, to escape the world of mothers and enter the world of fathers—to leave boyhood and step into manhood—requires an outward centrifugal masculine force strong enough to counter the inward centripetal feminine force. This is father energy: the energy of fathers and grandfathers and elders who, clearly, consciously, and ritually, initiate the boy into manhood.

Mothers can't do that. My mother couldn't do that. The best they can do is to recognize the necessity of father energy; and when it's time for initiation, the necessity of letting their boy go so he can find his rightful place in the community of men. The pain for both mother and boy is nearly unbearable, maybe the emotional equivalent of the mother's pain birthing that boy into the world. She, in one sense, is losing her boy; he, in one sense, is losing his mother. It feels like a death, and, in a sense, it is: the death of a boy and the birth of a man.

Son, I love your heart and your mind, your body and your soul. You are a beautiful boy. And you will become a beautiful man. I know there are things that you need from your father, and from other men, that I cannot give you. Don't worry about me. I will be here when you return. I release you on your journey to manhood.

BLESSING A CIRCLE OF MEN

Howard, Sam, & Fran

My father's friends were larger than life. They barely fit through our front door—all of them over 6' tall and 200 lbs, full of jokes and BS, full of love and hidden pain.

And full, too, of stories... Of my Dad driving a golf cart in Myrtle Beach, asking, "Are you with my, Howie?" "Always, Peter," Howard answered. At which point my father cranked hard to the right and drove the golf cart deep into a pond... Of Fran getting so angry he ripped a malfunctioning toilet right out of the bathroom floor, carried it across his front lawn, and dropped it by the curb... Of Super Bowl trips and hunting trips and golf trips... Of crossing the Atlantic in my father's tiny Cessna, hopscotching up through Greenland, ensconced in wet suits to keep them alive in the frigid waters should they go down....

They all had sons and daughters of their own. They all were sons of the Depression and WWII. They all were successful in a post-WWII American kind of way.

And they all loved my father.

These were not perfect men. One was a womanizer; one, a gambler. They were disconnected from their own deep anger, and sadness, and shame; disconnected from their own bodies. Pain, emotional or physical, was something they ignored or defeated. They, like my own father, were Unblessed sons themselves whose attempts to Bless their own sons and daughters were often crude and sometimes cruel.

But my father's friends were a blessing to my father, and they were a blessing to me. When they were around, my father was a different person. He relaxed, he softened. In the company of these robust men, my father was no longer someone I was afraid of: He was someone who told tall tales and set out on adventures. The sad, driven, isolated man vanished—and a beautiful, fun-loving boy burst out the front door to join his friends.

AA

I like a glass of good dry red wine with special dinners; I'll drink a beer every now and again; last October, I did too many shots of vodka at Jimmy's Polish wedding. That's about it. I've never had a drinking problem. I've never been in AA.

But I wanted to be.

In my late twenties I dated a cool woman who, several months into our relationship, told me she was an alcoholic and needed to deal with it. I said, Great, do what you need to do, and let me know how I can support you. She started going to AA meetings before work. She told me what they were like: all kinds of people from all kinds of backgrounds—black and white, street people, working-class and middle-class, teenagers and grandmothers—sitting around tables, smoking and drinking coffee, talking about their lives, sharing their stories, supporting each other.

That sounded wonderful to me. That sounded like an honest-to-god community; what church should be like, or therapy. America at its best, gritty and grace-filled.

I went to some Open Talks with her on Friday nights. Unbelievable. They blew me away. I had never heard anything like this before—this kind of raw honesty, this wide-open vulnerability. People doing exactly what most of us have been taught not to do: to put our pain out on the street, to strip off the shiny armor and bare our dark shadows. I sensed a serenity and a community here that I craved but knew no way of achieving.

No, I wasn't a drinker…or a drug-user, or a gambler. But I shared the hyper-sensitive, idealistic, perfectionist traits of many of those addicts, and I had my own addictions: "Hi, I'm Peter, I'm a Good Boy, I'm a Rescuer." So where the hell was I going to go to shed my shield and speak my truth? Where was my supportive community? Where was my AA?

I had already given up on the Catholic church. The air for me there was stale—people showing up, but still covered up, going through medieval motions. I needed more open heart, fresher spirit, more fire. Over the next decade, I threw myself into political organizations, relationships, Eastern religions. All gave me bits and pieces, but not a deep-felt feeling of connection. I was still a man alone—successful, well liked, but full of dark secrets and dim stories.

My AA—the organization I go to now for community, for shadow-sharing, for support—is the Mankind Project. The New Warrior Training Adventure weekend I attended on my 42nd birthday was a profound physical, psychological, emotional, and spiritual experience; so was the Warrior-Monk weekend I did several summers later. But the foundation of my program is my weekly Monday meeting with eight New Warrior men. Over the last four years, we have built a container of trust. We circle up in Joseph's basement and share our stuff—our secrets, our stories, our feelings. For two-and-a-half hours, we celebrate our lives as men; we honor our manhood.

Men need a special place they can go and speak their truth to each other. A place where they can safely unload their rage, own their fear, shed their tears, touch their shame, celebrate their joy. A sacred space where men can bless each other in the deepest, the holiest of ways.

Men, welcome to this space. Your anger is welcome here; so is your grief, your fear, your joy, and even your shame. I know it's hard to believe that. I know you feel that no container is strong enough to hold all the anger you have brewing in your body; that no container is thick enough to hold back all the sadness oceaned in your throat. I know that you are terrified to speak of your fear and your shame, especially to other men. I know it will take time to prove you will not be crushed for speaking your truth, but blessed. Take that time, take the risk. You are not alone, you will find out quickly that you are not alone. There is not one man in this space who hasn't felt ripped up and spit out; who hasn't felt paralyzed, stuck, empty; who hasn't felt lost and worthless. And there is also not one man in this space who doesn't have the seeds of strength and love in him; not one man, you included, who doesn't have everything he needs to be a strong, loving man. For this is the sacred space occupied by Warriors, Lovers, Magicians, and Kings. Welcome.

Guy Banter

Locker room talk, bar talk, phone talk. Guys shooting the shit, telling stories, telling lies, telling jokes. Quipping, ribbing, kidding. And sometimes, damn straight serious. Sports and cars, girls and music, trivia and theory—guys talking back and forth, around and around, sun up to sun down. "Reservoir Dogs," "Brothers McMullen," "Swingers," and "Diner" are chock full of it…Guy banter, that's what my wife calls it; and to her credit, she loves it almost as much as I do.

I grew up on guy banter. I listened to Howard, Sam, Fran and my dad kibitz, tell stories about golf trips and hunting escapades, mess with each other. There was something warmer and deeper than whatever they were actually talking about; it was the way these guys said "I love you."

In my late teens and early twenties, Brendan and I got together any time we could and traded "Theories." The Shipyard with its free cheese and crackers, a couple of Buds—and we were good to go, to talk, to theorize, to analyze, to solve our problems and the world's problems before closing time. Brendan was the master of sports metaphor; there was nothing he couldn't talk about through the lens of sports. If capitalism was going to work right, Brendan argued it had to be like the N.Y. Knick teams of the early 70s—"Distribute the ball more, make sure everybody gets a touch." In football and hoop, the offensive player's job was "creating some separation" between himself and his defender, which led to…"Guys are the offensive players—we're all about creating some separation—while women are all about closing the gap."

I loved those talks. Yes, we often theorized about "important" things in the world and in our lives—and that was cool—but as with my father's friends, there was something deeper going on here. At that time in our lives, Brendan and I were much more comfortable up in our heads, making up theories, than we were with our emotions. It was even a decade away from those "I love you, man!" commercials. But this is how we said it—over beer and crackers, through sports talk and sports metaphor, deep into the night.

Jimmy and I did it during college, the "I'm glad you're in my life-I'm glad you're my friend-I love you" disguised as guy banter. We traded self-deprecating barbs, he with the planet's deadest deadpan. Jimmy was my post-midnight moral advisor, helping me weigh the pros and cons of my sometimes-erratic behavior. It was Jimmy I called the night I ended up at the U Mass hospital after having eaten, unknowingly (I swear!), a whole plate full of marijuana-mixed brownies. While we shot baskets or played chess, we played with ideas and swapped life-lessons.

Men need guy banter. This is our oxygen, this is our glue. No, we don't do it like women; rather than heart-to-hearts, we're more comfortable with head-to-heads. But it's just as vital to us as it is to women. And underneath the banter, even if we don't say it or can't say it yet, the message is the same: I'm glad you're here, I'm glad we share what we share. My life is better because you're in it. I feel less lonely, more connected. I love you.

Both Brendan and Jimmy have been in my life for the past quarter-century. Though they live far away in New York and Poland, we continue our banter frequently over the phone and face-to-face several times a year. The talk these days is about children, as, miraculously, serendipitously, all three of us are having our first child at 45. I am blessed to have these men in my life, and I offer them a blessing.

Brendan and Jimmy, I thank you for all the years of talk, all the laughs, all the theories and queries and stories. Your company is tremendously important to me and my growth. I see you as strong, loving men, and I sense you see me the same way. So as one strong, loving man to two others, let me finally say what is beneath all the banter: I love you. Thank you for being there with me and for me—first as friends, now as fathers.

"Gentleman, welcome to Fight Club"

I'm 45-years-old, and I've never been in a fight.

That's a good thing, isn't it, never being in a fight?

Not according to Tyler Durden. Tyler, played by Brad Pitt in the film "Fight Club," says, "How much can you really know about yourself if you've never been in a fight?" So he asks Jack (Ed Norton's character) to wind up and hit him as hard as he can.

That's how the idea of Fight Club is born, and it spreads like wild fire. Seems like there's a whole generation of men like Tyler, Jack and myself who feel like we've missed out on something. Tyler's our leader; without pulling any punches, Tyler tells us who we are and how we feel:

> *We are the middle children of history, with no purpose or place. We have no great war, or great depression. The great war is a spiritual war. The great depression is our lives. We were raised by television to believe that we'd be millionaires and movie gods and rock stars—but we <u>won't</u> be. And we're learning that fact. And we're very, <u>very</u> pissed-off.*

Damn right I'm pissed-off!

And in my pissed-off state, if I could fight anyone...one on one, whoever I wanted, whom would I fight?

That's Tyler's question to Jack, and I've given Tyler's answer plenty of times:

> *My dad. No question.*

It's my favorite scene in the movie, Tyler scrubbing away in the bathtub as he delivers this line, Jack propped against a grungy wall on the bathroom floor, both of them talking fathers:

> JACK
> Oh yeah.
>   (nodding)
> I didn't know my dad. Well, I knew him, till I was six. He went and married another woman, had more kids. Every six years or so he'd do it again—new city, new family.
>
> TYLER
> He was setting up franchises. My father never went to college, so it was really important that I go.
>
> JACK
> I know that.
>
> TYLER
> After I graduated, I called him long distance and asked, "Now what?" He said, "Get a job." When I turned twenty-five, I called him and asked, "Now what?" He said, "I don't know. Get married."
>
> JACK
> Same here.
>
> TYLER
> A generation of men raised by women. I'm wondering if another woman is the answer we really need.

Maybe our fathers didn't know best. Maybe the times have changed, and we're on our own. Maybe we need to meet in basements on weekday nights with other men and talk about our fathers, fight our fathers, heal our wounds. Maybe we don't have to hit each other; maybe there's already been way more hitting than is good for us. Maybe this time around, we can break the conspiracy of silence and violence, and instead, do as a good King does, and bless each other.

Gentleman, welcome to Men's Club. The first rule of Men's Club is…tell other men about Men's Club. The second rule of Men's Club is—tell other men about Men's Club. The third rule of Men's Club is—tell yourself that you are a strong, loving man. The fourth rule—tell any man you care about that he is a strong, loving man.

The King's Round

On Monday nights in my men's group, we end with the King's Round. One of the most important functions of the King is to bless. To look over his kingdom and recognize the deep worth and effort he sees in people. The King speaks his Blessings, authentically, humbly, publicly.

Our current "Kings," our president, our leaders, Unblessed themselves, fail here. "God Bless America!" isn't sufficient.

And to be fair, we men have trouble on both ends here: on giving blessings, and receiving blessings. At best, we were raised on "Tough Love." Praise, to say nothing of blessing, was sissy stuff. Blessings were about as welcome as tears. Blessings were for church. The hard fact is many men, our fathers included, have Cursed us; and to defend our Unblessed selves, we have Cursed many men. So of course we're skeptical of anything that smacks of blessing.

One of the men in our group has really struggled with receiving blessings. "I don't trust it's really true," he says. "I think you want something from me." And given his history of a mother who manipulated him to get what she needed and a father who sexually abused him, it's not hard to see why he would be suspicious of blessings. But lately, after several years of resistance, during the King Round, his face, his whole body is more open, more receptive. When another man blesses him, I see his eyes take the blessing in; I see a small smile, a small nod.

Men need to be blessed by other men. I don't know if enough of these men's blessings add up to…The Blessing. I don't know if a circle of men authentically blessing each other can completely make up for what a father failed to do twenty or thirty or forty years ago. I do know it's powerful—one of the best salves for a man's father-wound. And I suspect it's one crucial step in a man's quest to be Blessed.

Son, I bless the Little Boy in you, I bless the Warrior in you, the Lover, the Magician, the King—all the beautiful parts of yourself. And all the parts of you that don't seem beautiful: your fear, your sadness, you anger, your shame. I bless you most of all for having the courage to speak your truth; and I'm here to tell you that when you do, no matter what that truth is, you are powerful and beautiful.

A Circle of Men

All these disconnected dots...Isolated rocks...Islands...Each one a man.

This is how we are supposed to live, we men. Alone, solo, heroic. A big part of being a man is cultivating the attitude and the behavior that I don't need other men. I can do it on my own. If I can't, I'm weak, a wimp, a loser. And behind that, since I've probably been burned by men—starting most tragically with my father—I don't trust men. It's better, *safer* to be a man alone.

There are brief respites, small, socially sanctioned arenas where men are allowed to leave their isolation and come together. Sports, for example. No wonder so many men (me included) get so damn excited over sports. We love the team chemistry, the locker room camaraderie, the connection. And, truth be known, we also get off on the *individualistic* side of sports—the incredible individual performances of a Jordan or an Armstrong or a Jeter. In that sense, sports sends us right back to our isolated "He's a Winner/I'm a Loser" selves.

And there are bars, places we men hope and pretend we'll find the likes of Norm, Cliff, Sam, Woody, and Frazier to share our lives with. To temporarily relieve us from our depressed, isolated existence...until Norm has to leave the sweet, high company of men and go home to his wife.

And sometime there is work where we can come together with other men and get something done, feel our power, shoot the shit—if we're not stuck alone in some cubicle or in some truck or behind some window.

Maybe there is church, although that is often man-to-God rather than man-to-man.

And of course, there is our family. We love our families, they love us back, and we do what we have to do to take care of them. But usually, there's only one man to a family—and sometimes the responsibilities of family get in the way of connecting with other men. The blunt truth is our families often don't and can't provide our lifeline to other men.

So where are the men in our life? Where are our authentic friendships with other men—men we can tell our joys and our shame to, our triumphs and our failures? Men we can trust our lives with—our *whole* lives, not just our physical bodies but also our deepest secrets?

We men have not always been so isolated. For thousands of years, we had no choice but to come together in order to survive. We gathered for the hunt and each man carried out his essential role during the hunt; and then we circled up around fires and told stories of that day's hunt and past hunts, of that day's hero, and past heroes—and maybe, of tomorrow's hunt and future heroes.

Where is *our* circle of men?

If I have a deep fear that I am not man enough—that I believe other men judge me not man enough—it is only other men who can confirm my Enoughness. To be healed of an Unblessed son's wounds, I must be seen, and heard, and hugged by a circle of men.

Where is my circle of men? I need a circle of powerful, loving men.
I can heal, if I can just get to a circle of men.

If I can drag myself out of my room, out of the bar, out of my car, out of the office, off my couch...and get to a circle of men.

Let me become part of that circle.
Let me join hands with other sons, other fathers, other brothers.
With other strong, loving men.

When it's my turn, let me stand in the middle of that circle.
Let me feel the love and power that a circle of men can provide.
Let that circle see me, hear me, hug me.
Let everything I am, all my shine and all my shadow, show.
Let me be the fire in the middle of that circle, and let me feel the fire of that circle.

Let me feel the healing power of a circle of men.
Let me feel the blessing power of a circle of men.
Let me remember again the ancient power of a circle of men.

Me and Seventy Men Had Ourselves a Weekend

Me and seventy men had ourselves a weekend
    where we closed our eyes
    opened our hearts
    descended into the pit of our fears
    and began the Hero's Journey...

Me and seventy men had ourselves a weekend
    where shards of fear, anger, sadness, shame, joy
    glittered like emeralds on a carpet

Me and seventy men had ourselves a weekend
    where our Little Boys leaped out of some dark corners
        and played for a second
        in the center
        of our circle

Me and seventy men had ourselves a weekend
    where we could look at a man younger than ourselves
    and say, Bless you for your age!
    where we could look at a man older than ourselves
    and say, Bless you for your age!

Me and seventy men had ourselves a weekend
    where "Thank you" was enough to bring a man to tears
    where "Thank you" meant thank you for bringing me
        to tears, or to fear, or to joy

where "Thank you" meant, I'll pass this on
    this is only the beginning.
where "Thank you" meant, "I love you"

Me and seventy men had ourselves a weekend
    where we invited a pack of wild animals
    and a troop of Wild men to help us along
    when the cave got too dark
    the pond too deep
    the cage too strong
    the pillow too heavy

Me and seventy men had ourselves a weekend
    where the fire raged from the center of the earth
    as a million Grandfathers and a thousand Brothers
        danced
    with strong arms & powerful legs & wild hearts
    to tell us these weekends had happened before,
    that we were warriors once
    and we are New Warriors now!

Me and seventy men had ourselves a weekend
    where we closed our eyes
    opened our hearts
    descended into the pit of our fears
    and made the Hero's Journey…

And when one of us climbed out the other side
    there were SEVENTY MEN waiting
    to take him to his King's chair
    and tell him truths he had always known
    but had somehow forgotten:
        As a man among men, I am not alone
        As a man among men, I am powerful

The Song of Father-Son

As a man among men, I am Blessed
and can Bless.

Me and seventy men had ourselves
one helluva weekend!

BLESSING OUR FATHERS

The Love Song of Father-Son

April, 1998. My father is lying in a South Carolina hospital with a ventilator plugged into his throat. He has no voice, this man who sang "Impossible Dream" in an impossibly deep bass, has no voice. Prone, a child. No longer 6' tall—no longer the frightening, booming, hair-cutting, wisecracking, story-telling giant of my childhood. A dying man in a hospital bed with no voice.

My mother, brother, and sister had left the room for the cafeteria. Just me and my father, alone, with a little bit of time.

How I had craved alone time with him. Six months before, he was supposed to meet me at the airport. Just him. We were going to go to California Dreaming for a sandwich before driving home to the rest of the family. I was dying for it; I couldn't remember a time when my father and I had had lunch alone. He liked my mom there, his surrogate feeler, his emotional buffer. But this time, alone, we would talk: this time, each of us would say whatever it was that father and son need to say to each other in order to heal and to bless...The plane landed; I pictured my father in the waiting area, habitually early, pacing, eager to get to the next place. You could count on it. When he wasn't there that November day—when I didn't see him in his green fall jacket and jeans, his keys swinging impatiently in his strong, sun-browned hand, I knew he was sick. And I was angry—angry at his sickness, yes, but especially angry because we would not have lunch alone together. Angry at him. Coward! I remember thinking. You who I once thought was afraid of nothing, so afraid to be alone with your thirty-eight year old son that you got sick!

Well, we were alone together now in this hospital room, but both of us were silent. Voiceless.

Then, his lips moved.

I blocked out the ventilator worming out of his throat and concentrated on his lips. Just his lips. They were thin and chalky, not his lips at all, but the lips of an old lonely dying man I didn't know. He was trying to say something, and I couldn't, for the life of me, understand him. I felt queasy pre-game jitters, stiffness, self-doubt. The mind-blanking panic that descends on me when, despite my five years of French, anybody speaks French to me: Je ne comprends pas! Je ne comprends pas! This was never going to work. At the best of times we had spoken different languages, my father and I: he talked guns and business, I talked peace and poetry. Usually, we had settled on sports heroes: growing up, Jim Brown & Arnold Palmer, lately, Barry Sanders & Tiger Woods. Great sons who spoke the language of athletic success—sons, I imagined, who made their distant deaf fathers proud.

Just his lips, just my father's thin, chalky lips were moving senselessly in the terrible whiteness of the room.

Once again, I was going to let my father down, and once again he was going to let his son down. So much to say, and no way to say it, to hear it, time running out.

But then, suddenly, miraculously, we both fell into this space, this sacred space, where my father was talking in a language I suddenly miraculously understood.

I'm sure the hospital hum continued—white ghosts walking in the hallway, machine purrs, TV crackle—but neither one of us noticed. Just this cool sacred space. Like the feeling of light entering some small Irish church. Or in a dream, we had entered the country of dreams, where flesh seems to be flesh—real son at end of real bed listening to real father—but something else too, mysterious and deep. And I was reading his lips as easily, as gracefully as I read a Mary Oliver poem or a "Hamlet" soliloquy.

Just his beautiful lips moving, making meaning.

"You've been having a dream?" I said.

He nodded fast. His lips moved again, quickened by my having understood.

"And you're not sure where it's from?" I said.

Yes, yes, he was nodding. His eyes were lighted with relief.

Then he told me about a boy, up in an attic, with something alive near the ceiling. High up, and frightening.

All those years of throated words and infinite time, and nothing, for either of us, ever, like this...This language, what would this language be called?

"I've been in that room," he lip-spoke.

"You've been in that room," I echoed.

"But I can't remember when," my father said. His lips, his face suddenly collapsed. I had never, in my life, seen him look as he did then: so lost, so terrified. So unimaginably alone.

A sliver of a story came back to me from my father's childhood. Alone on his birthday in some Upstate orphanage, his Depression-strapped parents temporarily out of resources. Was that the room, I wondered, somewhere in the bowels of that orphanage? And where had I heard that snippet from his childhood? Not from him, that's for sure. A great storyteller, my father only told certain kinds of stories—funny golf stories, crazy kid fights he and his brother got into it with the Lebowski twins down the block.

But not of scared little boys up in attics. My father didn't go there. Or maybe, I remember thinking, he had never left there.

"I've been in that room," *my father said again. He was seeing it again, clearly, and he was terrified. This, he now knew, was one mystery that would not be figured out with the tenacious, problem-solving intelligence he had applied to a lifetime of real estate deals and college education payments and trans-Atlantic plane trips.*

"I've been in that room," *I echoed.*

And then it struck me: I had, I had been in that room! Me too! I could suddenly see the boy, maybe six, thin and dark-haired—like my father as a boy, like me as a boy—peeking up into that deep, distant attic corner. To the blackness up there—what was it?—a balloon of sadness, or shame smeared across the ceiling like grape jelly. Suddenly, I didn't know where my father's dream, my father's emotions, my father's childhood ended and mine began.

My father raised his head from the pillow and looked at me closely. It had been a minute, a lifetime, since we had last spoken. I looked into his eyes now—he was talking with his eyes now. Did I understand? he asked. Did I get it? Was it OK to be afraid?

Now, it was my turn to nod.

Yes, I understood…Both of us were boys once…

Yes, I get it, Dad…scared to death, scared of death…

Yes, it's OK to be afraid…lost and now found, together, in this lonely room.

He relaxed his head back to the pillow and closed his eyes. And I felt tears, grateful tears rise in mine.

After almost thirty-nine years of noisy, anxious silence, we had spoken at last. Not about Willie Mays or taxes, but about what fathers and sons rarely speak of: our dreams and our fear, our sadness and our shame. Our death.

For a sacred moment, my father and I were fluent in the quietest, the deepest, the oldest of all the languages…Father-Son, the ancient, almost forgotten song of Father-Son…the language of the blood, where through some primordial umbilical cord of love, Father has always been—and will forever be—connected to Son.

Who's Your Daddy?

Any strong, loving man who looks you in the eyes and tells you,
You are a strong, loving man.

Go Gentle into That Good Night

As far as I know, my father was afraid of only two things: New York City, and death. Check that—one thing: He was afraid that if he went to NYC, somebody would kill him. So death, death was the only thing my father was afraid of.

Besides the usual angst aroused by death, my father had a terrifying experience when he was a boy. His sister tells the story of gentle Uncle John killed by WWII friendly fire and laid out to rest, open casket, in their home. My father had just turned nine, and it freaked him out.

Maybe it was from that day on that he made it his sworn duty to protect himself, and his kids, from death.

I was fourteen when my grandfather died. Gramps meant a lot to me: he was this hard-working little Italian man who saw me, heard me, blessed me in his own quiet way. I wanted to say good-bye to him. But my father wouldn't let me, or my brother and sister, go to his funeral. "They don't have to see this yet," he told my mother.

I saw my father cry twice, both at funerals—his mother's and his good friend's wife's. At his mother's, I thought his back was going to break from the violence of his soundless sobbing.

Then, at 63, my father got seriously ill. Over a four-month period he drifted toward death, spun slowly toward his end like a maple leaf spiraling down from the top branches toward the ground. My father lay in his hospital bed, strapped to machines, saddled with a lifetime of unexpressed fear, and stood watch as death came for him. I had never seen him so utterly helpless—and so mightily courageous. I saw him soften in those four months, let go, open up. I saw a frightened man arrive at some peace.

The last stanza of Dylan Thomas' "Do Not Go Gentle into That Good Night" had always moved me:

> And you, my father, there on the sad height,
> Curse, bless me now with your fierce tears, I pray.

> Do not go gentle into that good night.
> Rage, rage against the dying of the light.

But now, after watching my own father on his "sad height," I am grateful he did not go out raging. He lived fiercely, but died gently, and I feel blessed by his gentle tears.

Blessings My Father Did Give Me

I was nearly 40, and my father dead, before I fully realized he was one deeply insecure man. My father's fierce drive and physical strength, his quick mind and sense of humor, camouflaged a lot of fear and sadness and shame.

In my early 40s, I realized that to have expected such a blocked man as my father to give me The Blessing was unrealistic. Giving someone The Blessing is the most natural thing in the world—if you yourself feel like a strong, loving man. If you don't, if you have doubts about your strength, are locked into fear or anger or shame, blocked from love, then Blessing someone else is next to impossible.

Still, despite his own insecurities that blocked *The* Blessing, and my deep sadness and anger from not getting *The* Blessing, I recognize my father did manage to bless me in a multitude of ways:

I felt blessed to hang out with Howard, Sam, Fran—his funny, smart, male friends.

I felt blessed when I caddied for him and he asked me, "What do you think, seven iron or eight iron?"

I felt blessed by the patience he had while teaching me to drive.

I felt blessed by the letter he sent me my freshman year of college.

I felt blessed the time he told me he was proud of the courage it took to do my junior year abroad. "I know how much you enjoyed Amherst. I never would have left."

I felt blessed when I saw he was proud of all the knowledge I was soaking up from books and school. He never said it, but I saw it in his eyes.

I felt blessed when he said I was like Tim—"You're both good with people. People like you."

I felt blessed the day in Intensive Care when I read his lips like smoke signals, and both our worlds opened up.

I felt blessed when he told me the last time he had seen his own father before dying, BaPa had said good-bye to the both of us by calling my father what my father called me: Petey.

I felt blessed when my father died—as if he knew he had to go in order to give me the room I needed to grow into my own manhood.

No, finally my father did not have the capacity to give me The Blessing. UnBlessed and too wounded, he could not quite find the strength and love in himself to hug me and say, "Peter, you have all you need, all it takes, to be a strong, loving man."

And although I have moments at 45 where I still ache for his Blessing, I find myself more forgiving—more and more able to bless my father for all the blessings he *did* give his son.

Dad, you blessed me when you could, in the way you could. Thank you. I bless you for all those blessings, and for all the blessings I deeply believe you deeply wanted to give, but couldn't.

Sweet Forgiveness

Will I ever forgive my father for not giving me The Blessing?

Some days, it feels like I already have. Some days, I'm convinced that the sum of all his blessings…adds up to *The Blessing*. Some days, I'm completely clear on who he was—an Unblessed boy himself—and that he did the best he could.

And other days, less frequently of late, I'm furiously pissed at him for not fulfilling his fundamental duty as a father.

I'll be honest. Part of me wants to hold onto his failure. Part of me gets off on getting pissed, revving up my righteousness, writing poems about my pain. It's one of my most dynamic roles: Come see me strut my stuff as the VICTIMIZED SON! It's my version of those John Wayne westerns I watched with my dad as a kid: My father is the BAD FATHER, big and hairy and dressed in black from hat to boot; I'm the GOOD SON, lean and boyish and white right down to my underdrawers.

In those westerns, the BAD guy inevitably gets shot by the GOOD guy and bleeds all over the dusty street. Truth is, even on my most victim-fueled days, I don't want to shoot my dad. A well executed uppercut to the gut maybe—but no guns, no bullets, no blood. There's already been enough bleeding. I'm looking, these days, for some healing.

Dad, I'm tired of beating you up for not Blessing me the way I wanted to be Blessed. I want to honor you for all that you were, and not condemn you for things you couldn't be. Please forgive me for playing the GOOD SON, as I forgive you for playing the BAD FATHER. May this hug and these tears be the signs of our sweet forgiveness.

It's Not Your Fault: Take 2

It's not your fault.

I don't care how many times you hear it—"It's not your fault, it's not your fault"—you, like me, and like Matt Damon's character in "Good Will Hunting," may have trouble buying it.

Because chances are good that if you haven't received The Blessing, you will believe it *is* your fault. Everything. The whole mess your life is, and the whole mess the world is.

Either that, or maybe you'll believe NONE of the mess is your fault. It's all HIS fault, your FATHER'S fault!

Well, it's not your fault *and* it's not, finally, your father's fault either.

Which is far less comforting some days than it should be. Because some days, I just want to beat myself up: *Asshole, you fucked up again, you're incompetent, you're weak—when are you going to get your shit together?!* I just want to pound away again on Pitiful Me. And some days, I just want to blame my father for everything not working perfectly in my life: *Asshole, if you had just given me the goddamn Blessing, I wouldn't be so fucked up, and everything would be perfect!* I just want to wail, whine, and wallow in my victimhood.

But the painful truth is, it's not my fault—because I didn't get The Blessing; and it's not my father's fault—because he didn't get The Blessing either. And most likely, the same is true for you and for your father.

So if it's not our fault, and not our father's fault—whose fault is it?

Maybe the fault lies with the word "fault." Maybe trying to pinpoint whose fault it is keeps us from healing. Maybe it's just a matter of someone stepping up and stepping through the pain; some son breaking the cycle by standing up and giving The Blessing—to himself, to his father, to his son, to the boys and men in his life.

I hereby give myself The Blessing my father was unable to give me, and The Blessing his father was unable to give him: I am a powerful, loving man, and I see the power and love in you, Dad; and in all the boys and men who are presently in my life, in all who will cross my path, and in all future sons, should they come. From this point on, I am a Blessed son surrounded by Blessed sons.

"Sometimes You Can't Make It On Your Own"

This U2 song has been in my head for days. It opens with clicking percussion, an acoustic guitar, and Bono's weary, tender voice beside, I imagine, his father's deathbed:

> *Tough, you think you've got the stuff*
> *You're telling me and anyone*
> *you're hard enough.*

The son is softening, offering:

> *You don't have to put up a fight*
> *You don't have to always be right*
> *Let me take some of the punches*
> *for you tonight.*

Sudden crescendo—swelling background music, the son's voice desperate now, trying to break down forty years of stony toughness while there's still time:

> *Listen to me now*
> *I need to let you know*
> *You don't have to go it alone*

Then falsetto—the high point of the song—the son recognizing he's the spitting image of his father, and just as disconnected:

> *And it's you when I look in the mirror*
> *And it's you when I don't pick up the phone*

Back to the son's deeper, fuller voice for the title line:

Sometimes you can't make it on your own.

I think that line, "Sometimes you can't make it on your own," is meant for both father *and* son. The father has been going it alone for his whole life, is still going it alone as he approaches death, tough to the end. Ditto for the son: he, too, has been going it alone for years without a deep, direct connection to his father, and it's been tough, made him tough.

But the son has a new truth he wants to share with his father—I need you now, and you need me now. Apart, we're homeless, we hurt. Neither one of us can make it on our own:

> *Where are we now?*
> *I've got to let you know*
> *A house still doesn't make a home*
> *Don't leave me here alone....*

The son now knows, too, where his incredible music comes from—from his father, from their silence and their pain, right from the heart of their ancient, deep wound. And in telling his father that, whether or not he is heard, he gives his father and himself The Blessing:

> *Can-you-hear-me-when-I*
> *sing, you're the reason I sing*
> *You're the reason why the opera is in me....*

My Father's Eulogy

My father's eulogy is one of the best things I've ever written.

All the time he was in Intensive Care, days and days, weeks, I resisted the urge to begin writing it. My notebook was right there in my knapsack, under the chair, behind the hospital bed he was lying on. I wanted the comfort that words bring me. The control. I wanted to get it right. I wanted to find a way to say in writing what neither one of us had ever quite managed to say aloud.

But I read to him instead. I read his lips. I held his hand. I rubbed oil on his shoulders and back.

And when he finally died, I sat at my parents' computer for ten hours straight and wrote his eulogy.

In it, I captured my father's irrepressible drive, his zinging wit, his hyperactive love, his enduring friendships. I ended with Hamlet's words about his father, the dead King: "He was a man, take him for all in all,/I shall not look upon his like again."

Did I get it right? Did I find the words to Bless the both of us?

That quote from *Hamlet* is from early in Act I. Hamlet hasn't even hooked up with the ghost of his father yet, much less avenged his murder. It takes him four soul-tossed, soul-testing Acts before this son throws off his sadness and his anger and becomes a man. Before this prince becomes a King.

I had some work to do too.

When my father passed seven years ago, I had never heard of The Blessing. I hadn't yet written two dozen poems about my father, about my anger, about the fights we never had when he was alive. I hadn't read any Jung, or done any therapy yet. I hadn't yet perused my dreams for truths—wasn't even aware I *was* dreaming. I hadn't yet been on my New Warrior weekend. I hadn't even met Julia, much less married her; and I wasn't expecting my first child.

In short, although I was almost 39 when I delivered his eulogy, I was still a boy. An Unblessed son who did his best to bless an Unblessed father.

Dad, I still treasure your drive, your humor, your awkward love. I now see much more clearly the deep sadness beneath your anger. I forgive you for not Blessing me, as you were not Blessed. And my wish is that we could hug now for the first time—as father and son, as friends, as men. As Kings.

BLESSING FATHERHOOD

Six Years Soon

◆

(On the 6th anniversary of my father's death)

Look at me now!
How fast I've grown!
Look at how beautiful I've become!
Look at my wife, my heart, my home.

When you died
and I sprinkled words over you
something took seed in me
and I've watered that soil
with tears
and worked that soil
with anger.
And I'm crying now
as I write new words
these words
and sprinkle them
like blessing
on myself.

And now for the first time
I feel how life
rises from death,
how a father
gives birth
to a son.

What Will I Be When I Grow Up?

I pondered that question at 10. At 20. At 30. At 40. What will I be when I grow up? It's a damn good question for a boy to ponder.

"When I grow up" implies I'm presently small. I'm a kid—over there, Grown-ups. And what those Grown-ups are doing is Important. They are not wasting their time, wasting their lives. They have a Goal, a Mission, a Plan, and they are executing it. They are doing what they were put on this earth to do.

But when I was 10, and I looked around, I couldn't say for sure that anybody was really doing what they were born to be doing. Most Grown-ups just seemed to be living, surviving. Even my father, who with his fanatical discipline and drive, was accomplishing things—he won the Edison Club Championship in golf, he started his own business, he was learning to fly—didn't seem to have some grand Goal. He was winging it just like the rest of us.

When I was 20 and about to graduate from a prestigious college, poised to enter the best that Grown-up life had to offer, I looked around again. Mostly, I saw a lot of kids playing—playing at careers, playing at parents, playing at politics. Or maybe that was my projection: despite my academic success, despite my urgent desire to do something Big, I still felt small. I was a boy heading off to teach other boys at an Academy.

By the time I was 30, I thought I had The Answer, found out the Big thing I was destined to do in this world. Family, friends, poetry, sports…insignificant, irrelevant. I was a revolutionary. I was going to change the whole world. I woke up most mornings feeling like I had a Mission. I was so intense, so immersed in my Mission, my scared little boy went underground.

When I hit 40, I was distraught. My revolutionary zeal had withered. The scared little boy had emerged again and found himself staring at the same goddamn question: What was I going to do when I grew up? But some things had changed. My father had died the year before. I had watched him grow up in the last several months of his life; strapped to a hospital bed, unable to use his prodigious energy to run anymore, he was forced to face his own life and death. I now found my dreams were telling me truths my brain couldn't. I had finally left a debilitating, rescuing relationship, and had met Julia.

And another, related question had surfaced: What does it mean to be a man? Looking back now, I think that was the actual question from the beginning—not "What will I be when I grow up?" but more specifically, "What does it mean to be a man?" That it took me thirty years to refine my question to this tells me how lost I was all those years.

At 45, married, a baby due in June, I have a tentative answer to that new question, What does it mean to be a man? A man stays and faces his shadow—his demons, his dreams, his addictions, his gifts, his parents. A man learns to love his shadow. A man finds someone else to love.

In short, a man does King's work, Father's work: He Blesses—himself, his parents, his partner, his children, his friends, his neighbors, his world.

Legacy

My wife and I saw the musical "Rent" last night. Roger is one of its main characters, a dying HIV-infected rock singer in his mid-twenties. Early on, he's holed up in his New York City apartment, clutching his guitar like it's god. Softly, sadly, he sings, "I just want to write one great song before I go…"

Julia tapped me on the shoulder. "Legacy," she whispered.

She knows me well. I was already scooted up in my seat, drawn to Roger's end-of-life plight. She knows that I have been obsessed with my own legacy since I was in diapers: What great thing am I going to leave behind? After I die, what of me will live?

Legacy, it seems to me, is much more a men's question. A men's obsession. Women don't seem nearly so caught by it, caught up in it. Maybe it's because a woman has the potential to create the future right out of her own body—the real McCoy, real flesh and real blood, babies with tiny toes and clutchy fingers and burpy smiles that will eventually, if all goes well, grow into men and women who will be alive long after the woman has passed on. Her legacy.

Yes, we men are necessary to the whole birth thing, but we're tangential. Or we often feel we are. Crudely, it's three or four seconds of seed-squirting for us, and nine months of rooting, growing, nurturing, gardening for women. You take our small idea—and run with it, give it arms, legs, heart, brain. Life.

So we feel compelled to come up with some big ideas of our own, something to match your wondrous, miraculous gift of life. If I'm a male writer, and I can write a great novel, my characters and their story will live on long after I'm gone. The same with a great painting, or a building, or a business: men's attempts to birth something beautiful that will outlive us. *Our* legacy.

In my own life, I was damn sure my legacy would be created far from home and hearth. The home was women's territory; I would birth my baby in some lonely writer's room or on some noisy street corner atop my revolutionary soapbox or in some pristine desert or on some clean mountain peak.

And maybe I will. But more and more these days I find myself closer to home, and being OK with that. I've come to see and believe that my parental role here could be more than squirt-and-run; that if it takes a village to raise a child, that village better have some strong, loving fathers, some male elders. And I could be one of them.

We men feel like we're not enough. We are afraid that we will live our whole lives and have nothing beautiful to show for it. We often feel wounded, worthless, wombless, Unblessed.

Son, I sense how restless you are to create beauty in your life, beauty that will outlive you. I honor that instinct, and I can also tell you you can relax. You have all you need to be a strong, loving man; and out of your strength and your love, naturally, inevitably, you will create beauty—beautiful art, if you choose, beautiful organizations, beautiful children. Trust me, yours is a King's legacy.

Martha's Vineyard

Several months before my wedding, Jimmy and I went to Martha's Vineyard. Jimmy's one of my greatest friends, and we've been making jokes, playing chess and hoop, and talking about our lives for the last twenty-five years. This was our third or fourth summer in a row that we had carved out a long weekend on the Vineyard to sit back and catch up. It was my version of a bachelor party—just me and Jimmy and all the intimacies that two thoughtful, growing 44-year-olds can bring to the table.

Some of the talk, of course, was about marriage. But a lot of that had been covered the previous summer, after my proposal. The hot scary new topic was children.

Neither one of us had any. Jimmy had always assumed he would—and in about a month from now, he will—but right then, single, with no good woman in sight, it was still a pretty abstract proposition. I, on the other hand, had been beating myself up for at least the last ten years: Could I be a father? What would I lose, what would I gain? What does it mean to be a good father? That guy over there, cleaning ice cream off his two-year-old's face, what was he thinking—that fatherhood is the greatest thing in the world, exactly what I should be doing in this life...or what the hell have I gotten myself into?

I still didn't know, and I told Jimmy that.

Now, the thing you got to know about Jimmy is that he's a problem-solver. In fact, in a world where most men are men because they problem-solve, James Van Bergh, with his amazingly agile mind and his big heart, is one of the best. He's almost *too* good sometimes. One sentence out of your mouth—and Jimmy's got three scenarios, two recommendations, and a $100 bill to help you on your way.

But that summer, on this topic, he surprised me. We were sitting in lounge chairs on the Tivoli Inn porch, sipping on orange juice while the June morning unfolded around us. And when I launched into my deep ambiguity about having children, instead of juicing up his left-brain and cranking out possible "answers," Jimmy just listened.

I told him I was angry. At my father, mostly, for being too strong, too severe with us. For making us afraid of him. For not telling me he was proud of me.

And for making it impossible for me to just flat-out hate him, which would have been easier.

I told him I was afraid. Afraid I wouldn't be the perfect parent who said the perfect, healing thing each and every time. Afraid I wouldn't have the patience. Afraid I'd try so hard not to be my father, try so hard to be only loving, only caring, only praising—that I'd end up blowing-up, and my kids would fear me just like I had feared my father.

It felt good to say it all, especially to another man. It felt good to be heard.

The next morning, Jimmy came to breakfast and handed me a card. On the front was a beautiful photo of a sculpture called the "Flute Player"—a lilting, tilting, flying-fingered musician with a Tom Sawyer hat and a woman's soft, bread-rising belly. The day before, after our talk, we had wandered among a dozen of these life-sized, white-stoned figures at the Field Gallery in Chilmark. On the inside of the card, Jimmy had carefully written the key points of an "image" that had come to him upon awakening. "It's weird," he said, "because this didn't feel like anything 'rational.' It didn't seem like I had thought it up. But it feels true, I can say that much."

Here's what the card said. Here was The Blessing my great and wise friend bestowed on me on our latest pilgrimage to Martha's Vineyard:

My Image

I imagine that through your children, you will:

*—relive the power and love
your father bestowed on you*

*—recover the peace and gentleness
that was stolen from your father*

*—release the "ball of anger" which
blocks you from finding and expressing
your truth.*

Present Dads

I am extremely grateful that my father never physically abandoned me or my family. He was there day-in, day-out, working and worrying his butt off, paying the bills. I know a lot of men whose dads did leave. And the father energy left with them.

But just because my father was there didn't mean he was present. He was, much of the time, a present/absent dad: physically there, but emotionally disconnected.

Back then, he wasn't allowed to come into the labor and delivery room and be present at my birth, and I'm not sure he would have been able to handle it if he could have come in. He paced out in the waiting room, smoked cigarettes, stared down the clock. In a sense, he was in that waiting room our whole life together: he never found the way to step through the door—to step through his own fear, pain, shame, sadness—and come into my room. The best he could do—and I thank him for this, too—was to peek in and close my door at night. I asked him once why he did that, closed our doors. An insurance salesman by trade, he told me that in case of fire, a closed door would give someone ten more minutes of time. My father was a protector, not a nurturer; despite his best intentions, he operated out of fear, not love. And his fear kept him absent.

What I craved was a present dad. A dad who saw me, heard me, hugged me, honored me. A dad who had worked through enough of his own jumbled, childhood stuff to be emotionally connected to his son.

I am pleased to report I know a number of present dads: Sam, Don, Rick, Rich, Jeff, Billy, Michael S., Michael M., Brendan, Jimmy. I think that's the wave of the future, dads who were present at the births of their children, and who stay present. Not every minute, not every day—but much more often than not, they are there to see and hear and hug and honor.

Dads, thank you for modeling what it means to be present for your sons and daughters. In you, I see the strong, loving father I wanted for myself—and the strong, loving father I want to be for my son.

BLESSING OUR WORLD, BLESSING OUR FUTURE

My Father's Grave

I've always been a fan of cremation. I love the idea of ashes sprinkled from atop mountains or over meadows or into oceans... Ah, free at last, free at last!

But when my father died, and instead of cremating him, we buried him, as he wished, in Oconee, South Carolina, I was glad.

His grave is in a cemetery under a large pine tree a quiet distance in from the road. In the seven years since his death, I've returned there maybe a half dozen times. Once with my mother and seven-year-old nephew, William: I made up a Grandpa game that we played together beside the grave, and all of us laughed, though I was crying too. Another time with my mother, brother, and Julia: Julia took a picture of the three of us loosely hugging by the base of the pine, not facing the camera, smiling through some tears.

But I like it best when I go alone. I lean against the tree and twirl a pine needle in my hand. Or I squat on one side or the other of the now-seeded dirt. I guess I think a little bit about the past, and I'm sure I talk some, sometimes even aloud, but I'll be damned if I know what I've said. I always cry, sometimes hard tears, usually soft. I cry and I just feel my father's presence.

When alive, my father was always on the move, a nearly maniacal Energizer Bunny. I like that he's resting now—here, in one spot—so I can be this close to him for an hour or so.

When I visited last summer, I sat cross-legged right on the heart of his grave. It was a beautiful July day, his birth month—sun-warmed grass and blue air everywhere. Peaceful, I felt peaceful, seeing and not seeing the in-laid headstone in front of me: Peter H. Putnam Sr./1934–1998.

A flicker of something caught my eye. In the shadows of another pine tree a hundred feet in front of me—a crow, a big, shinydark crow directly across from where I was sitting. This crow, the first and only of the day, was hip-hopping all around the largest upright headstone in sight. I could easily read its carved name: **KING**.

The week before in my men's group I had taken a new animal name for myself—Holy Crow; and the last thing we do in our meeting is the King's Round—the Blessing round. Call me crazy, but I felt a bona fide Blessing right then and there while sitting atop my father's grave: this holy King crow blessing these two formerly Unblessed sons, my father and me, and blessing our continued life together.

Now What?

At one point, I wasn't sure there was much hope for those of us who didn't get The Blessing from our fathers. I felt like I would never be strong enough, loving enough—man enough. I would forever be the weak son of a giant, absent father.

But, really, that was all before I even consciously knew about The Blessing. When in October, 2001, at the Michigan Fathers Conference, local therapist and New Warrior Tom Fitzpatrick outlined his ideas of The Blessing, I felt immediately, well, blessed: I suddenly understood why I still felt like a boy and what the hell I had been searching for all those years. It was like finally being given the diagnosis to the mysterious illness that for decades had pained me, plagued me terribly. I wasn't instantly healed; there was a lot of work—the "treatment"—to be done. But now at least I had my hands around something my head and heart agreed was the key missing piece.

Now what? Tom had some concrete ideas. He said it was absolutely essential for a man who had tremendous father-hunger to "get some of that father." For there can be no Blessing without Father, without Father-energy.

But where would these pieces of Father come from?

From each other, Tom said, from men: from male kinship systems (brothers, cousins, uncles, grandfathers); from elders; from men's groups (like the Mankind Project, for instance, or local groups like the Men of Today and F.A.T.H.E.Rs Forum). Here were men who could perhaps give us the essence of The Blessing: approval; acceptance of our strengths *and* our weaknesses; assurance of our purpose, our Mission—as well as help in creating that Mission and the permission to pursue it; and finally, knowledge of how to be a man—men teaching men how to be strong and loving by example, by walking the walk.

At that time, I had ten new men in my life from my New Warrior Weekend three months earlier. We were meeting once a week, just getting to know each other, just beginning to experiment with some of the skills, tools, and processes we had been exposed to briefly on the Weekend, and then had been taught to us in an eight-week, post-Weekend "Integration training." This was my "I-Group," my men's group. Here was a space where I could feel the approval of men; where

I could explore my gold and my dark shadow; where I could be challenged to forge and live my Mission. Here was a big piece of Father.

And outside of our I-group, in the Detroit-Windsor Mankind Project community, there were a number of men and elders I could look to see how a strong, loving man walked in the world: Steve, Tim N. and Tim B., Ralph, Rich, Ed, Wayne, Ross. These were Blessers of men—more pieces of Father.

My brother, Paul. My long-time friends, Brendan and Jimmy and Sam and Don. My brother-in-law, Billy. I began seeing these men with different eyes. I wanted deeper connections with them. I wanted to share what I was learning about my own masculinity, my son-ness, and I wanted to hear their thoughts and feelings on men, sons, and fathers. These were further shards of Father—and The Blessing Fathers can give.

And then there were my own dreams. My father, who had died in 1998, appeared here regularly: asleep in a pilotless plane, stuck in an airport wheelchair, racing me through a dark parking lot to my Subaru. And then one hugely significant dream where I had the side of my boy's face pressed into his chest, his arms around me, mine around him, hugging. Other dreams not specifically with my father, but with father figures, powerful men—coaches, mostly, professors, a doctor. Internal images—nighttime bits of Father, midnight whispers of Blessing.

I worked with these dream images, and the images that arose in my writing and my poetry. Using what Jung called active imagination, I cobbled together my own enactment of The Blessing: I feel the strength of my father's arms around me in that dream image; I feel the warmth of his sweater, hear his strong, steady heart beat—and his words: "Petey, you have all you need to be a strong, loving man." Again: "Petey, you have all you need to be a strong, loving man." One more time, slower, deeper, as he moves me away from his chest and looks down into my eyes: "Petey. You have all you need to be a strong…loving…man." I can see the sheen of tears in his eyes through the shimmer of my own tears, hear the catch of love in his throat. Dream Fathers, The Blessing spun from night dreams and daydreams and prosedreams.

And I'm about to embark on what I have been told—by Fitzpatrick, by Frank Pittman, by countless men—is the richest source of Father: Fatherhood. If all goes well, in less than five months, at forty-five years of age, I will become a father. I will have the opportunity to Bless a son or a daughter—and, in what seems a miraculous reciprocity, to be Blessed. I've already started: Each night I lay my hand on my wife's blooming belly and say the words, "Son, you have all you need to be a strong, loving man," and, since we don't know the sex, and since I believe The Blessing is also a daughter's birthright, "Daughter, you have all you need to be a strong, loving women." If I continue this Blessing through birth, then childhood, and into adolescence and beyond, I am quite certain my children will feel they have a strong, loving father—and I will feel like a strong, loving man myself. I will have given, and received, The Blessing I have been craving all of my life.

There are things a man can do to receive The Blessing his father was unable to give him. He can find the necessary pieces of Father in his family and friends; in men's groups; in leaders; in dreams; in books and poems; in his own imagination. Most of all, he can be a father himself—to his own son or to the millions of scared boys in the world, sons of all ages, who want nothing more than The Blessing from a strong, loving man.

In so doing, in so gathering, in so giving, a fatherless Unblessed boy is finally Blessed.

Sons, do not despair. Your father may be dead, or disappeared, or indifferent. You may have long ago given up on getting The Blessing, or you might still be looking everywhere for The Blessing. You may not only be fatherless, but friendless; Missonless; leaderless; childless. But finally, you are not alone: there are millions of men who feel the father-loss you feel. Find some of these men and begin to piece together the puzzle of Father with them. Gather other pieces from your dreams, your reading and your writing, your imagination. Create the Father you need to give you The Blessing you crave. And finally, pass The Blessing on: find boys who are like you once were, Unblessed boys, and tell them what you now know about yourself: Trust me, Son, you have all you need to be a strong, loving man.

This is how we change the world—one Unblessed son at a time.

A Man's Mission

What do you want most? What are you doing to get it?

A man needs a Mission. Without a conscious Mission, a man can easily be sucked into the hole of his addictions, and his "Mission" then becomes to satisfy those addictions. Honestly answering these two questions can begin to give a man some clarity about his true Mission.

What do you want most? What are you doing to get it?

Growing up, what I wanted most was my father's Blessing. Here are some of the things I was doing to get it: straight "A"s, baseball and basketball star, "Please" and "Thank you."

There's a third question a man can ask to clarify his Mission: How is that working for you? OK, you have this **Vision** (What do you want most?) and you're taking this **Action** (What are you doing to get it?)—now, how is that working for you? In other words, are you getting what you want, and how do you know that?

How was that working for me, my Mission of wanting my father's Blessing and being the All-American Good Son to get it?

For the first half of my life, it seemed to be working wonderfully. I went to a great college, and then a great grad school, and then I got a great job and had a handful of relationships with great women. Being an All-American Good Son definitely has its perks.

But did I get my father's Blessing? No.

Did I still want my father's Blessing? Yes.

Meanwhile, I continued to perform my role as the All-American Good Son. In fact, more accurately, I attempted to be the All-American Good *Father* I had always wanted—present, caring, listening, blessing. I attempted to be *every*body's All-American Good Father…

How was that working for me?

It wasn't. I was drained. In my late thirties, I bottomed out. I needed a new Mission.

Over the last four years, through the Mankind Project and its New Warrior weekend, through my men's group that came out of my weekend, and through my persistent attempts to clarify what was most important in my life and to take the necessary action to achieve that vision, I have lived my way through several new Missions. The latest version, I am proud to say, took shape this morning, right here, as I wrote this piece:

My Mission is to create a world of Blessed sons by Blessing myself, Blessing my father, Blessing my brother, and Blessing each son who crosses my path.

And in fact, writing this book, *The Song of Father-Son,* is one of the things I am doing to create such a son-Blessed world.

I am excited about this fresh Mission. Joyful. Like many sons who do not receive The Blessing from their father, my "Mission" for much of my life has been directly or indirectly connected to winning his Blessing. I am more and more ready to let go of that attempt, to let go of the addictions that arise from it. I am on the path of Blessing my father, of trusting that a circle of men can also Bless me; and of knowing that, in order to avoid burning out, I must find and feel the power and love to Bless myself in order to have the power and love to Bless other men.

Son, I am proud of your Mission. You have discovered what you want most in this world, and you are taking the steps to bring your deepest desire to life. Your vision and your actions give me hope. I see you as a man with a powerful, loving Mission joining other men with powerful, loving Missions. Together, you are creating a powerful, loving planet.

The Power of a Son's Imagination

None of what I've written below actually, literally happened. Some are dramatic rewritings of Cursed moments; some are capturings of missed moments; some are loosely tied to a specific place or time; some are the refined pieces of dream. All of them are demonstrations of the power of my imagination to create The Blessings from my father I have so long craved.

There is a ton of research—Maxwell Maltz's *Psycho-Cybernetics*, for one, which I read when I was a teenager—that shows that the mind cannot distinguish something that has been vividly imagined from something that has "literally" happened. So here's what I can do: with a grateful nod to Jung and his development of "Active Imagination," I can slip into the infinite depth of my unconscious and let some of those Blessings bubble up; I can write them down, "see" them happening in my mind's eye, play them out when I'm doing my morning run or in front of a mirror or anytime during the day.

In the short term, I've experienced a tearful, quickening joy when playing these images on the CD of my imagination. Long term, I believe I will more and more feel—deeply, in my body—like the Blessed Son I have always wanted to be.

I'm on my father's shoulders, riding high, a giant bouncing through the world. My hands play in his thick black hair, his strong hands hug my ankles.

We're up in the dormer room on Cortland Dr. looking out the window at the bedtime darkness and an emerging moon. We have our hands around each other's backs, and we're both singing, "When the moon hits your eye like a big pizza pie, that's amore!" with exaggerated swaying and emphatic Italian hand gestures.

My father and I are playing pitch-and-catch in the backyard. He drops down into a catcher's squat; I go into an extensive wind-up and fire him my best ten-year-old fastball. "Striiiiiike!" he says. And when he throws me an "I'm proud of you" smile back with the ball, the summer evening light fills my body like a song.

The side of my face is up against the softness of his cashmere sweater; my arms are around him has far as they can stretch; his arms circle securely all the way around me. I can smell his faint sweat and hear his strong, steady heart as I ride the gentle waves of his breath.

I tell a funny joke and my father laughs really, really hard—his high cheekbones pulled back, his teeth all-aglitter, his belly bouncing. He even slaps the arm of his brown leather chair with his left hand.

The backyard is alive with late morning spring sun. I hear the sweet snip of scissors—my hair tickling as it tumbles to the earth. Black-capped chickadees watch from the apple tree above us, waiting to feather their nests with tufts of my soft hair. My father's strong, warm hand is on the top of my head, and I feel safe, connected, handsome.

We're showering side-by-side in a locker room. My father is big, hairy, and 35; I'm small, hairless, and 10. While soaping up, he sees me looking curiously and nervously at his penis; smiles. "Your penis will be just as big as this some day, and you'll have hair all over your body, just like me." "Really?" I ask, because his penis looks like a whole other species from mine, and I can't imagine where all that hair is going to sprout from. "Really," he says. "You've got everything you need to be a man." Now I smile, and he passes me the soap.

We're in a field, walking side-by-side, sun just tipping above the horizon. I'm chilly but warm at the same time. This field is bursting with partridge and pheasant and maybe even a woodcock or two. The shotgun in my hands is a thousand years old. My father is Hunter, and I am his Son.

My father is waist-deep in a bright, clean outdoor pool. He smiles and invites me to dive in with a "I'm right here" and a gesture of his hands that moves like the first stages of a hug. I take two steps, slam my eyes shut, and launch myself water-ward. Go under. Angry bubbles all around me. I panic for a second. Then feel his hands pulling me up to air, to safety, to him.

I'm in my mother's womb, floating, riding low. I hear percussive circling and I feel magnetic energy from just above my head: his hand rubbing, his words finding their way through the thick fluid I'm pickled in: "Son, you have all you need to be a strong, loving man."

We're boxing, my father and I, in the family room. All the furniture is pulled back. I'm snapping left jabs into his open hand. He shows me how to throw a right. "Like this," *he says,* "from the shoulder." *I try it.* "That's it! Now try this: jab, jab, right." *I do* "Jab, jab, right!" *toward his chin—and my father weaves, wobbles...and falls with a slapstick crash on the couch. I dance around the room scissoring my legs like Ali and pumping my arms over my head in celebration.*

My grandfather has just died, and I'm up in my room with the door closed. I can feel my sadness like a dead weight in my chest, but I'm not crying, I can't cry. My father knocks and comes in. He sits on the edge of my bed. "It really hurts, doesn't it?" *he says. I see tears in his eyes; he loved my grandfather too. I nod and look away.* "It's OK to cry," *he says.* "He was a good man, and we're going to miss him." *And that's all I need to hear—I break into hard sobbing, and my father holds me in his arms until the tears slow and the dead weight in my chest dissolves.*

Prom day. I'm in tux and shiny black shoes. My father puts his hands on my shoulders; we're almost eye-to-eye. "I'm proud of you." *Hands me the keys to the car.*

July. Galway Lake. I'm solo in the rowboat, shirtless, bare feet, fourteen. My father pushes me off from shore; he gives me a broad smile and waves good-bye. I smile and wave back without letting go of the oar. Then I dip both oars in the water and pull, hard, with my back and shoulders, and push, hard, with my legs. I glide gigantically toward the middle of the lake. My father is still there, standing on the shore, not waving anymore, just watching, watching me move away, and I feel his Blessing ripple across the water and settle in my chest.

Lying in bed between my Little League sheets, I hear his footsteps coming up the stairs...then down the hallway. He's at my door now. Through sleepy eyes I see him peek in and find me. Then he slowly begins to close the door. As the light fades, I hear his soft, deep voice like a prayer: "Son, I'm so proud of you. Sleep tight." *And what I feel running all through me is shiny as gold, only softer, soft as cashmere, and I sleep like a baby.*

My father is lying between hospital sheets. He's got a tube in his throat so he can't talk. I read his lips: "Son, I'm proud of you," *then he closes his eyes and sleeps like a baby.*

Your Father's Blessing

Have you slowed down in your life long enough to answer this essential question: Growing up, what did you want your father to say to you? What words did you crave from him? What words from him were you dying to hear—and are still dying to hear? What words from him could bring some healing, some foundation, some freedom?

Now, if you're ready and you haven't already done so, is a good time to bring those words to life—to receive The Blessing from your father.

Close your eyes. Listen inside. What you wanted your father to say to you, what you still want your father to say to you, is right there, available, ready for you to wrap words around. I'll give you some possibilities in a minute, but I don't want to get in your way. You already know. You already have it. It's inscribed in your heart. You've been mouthing it in dreams for decades. You know it as well as you know your own name.

Close your eyes, go inside, and find that now, find those words, those healing words.

And, if you're ready, here's the space to write those words down; the next step to making your father's Blessing real—*Write his words for you right here, right now*:

Here are other ways you may want to experience your father's powerful, healing Blessing:

Find a private mirror and say your father's words to yourself into the mirror. Say them aloud, if possible. Say them again. And again. And maybe again.

> *"Petey, I'm proud of you."*
> *"Son, it wasn't your fault."*
> *"Terry, you're handsome and smart and I'm sorry."*
> *"Mike, you can rest now."*

Let come up whatever comes up—sadness, anger, shame, forgiveness, love.

Have your wife, or partner, or friend say these words to you. Close your eyes. Take them in. Allow whatever comes up for you to come up. Witness it. As much as possible, relax into it.

Choose a man who carries something of your father's energy or appearance. He might be your best friend or somebody you barely know. Have this man say the words…say them again…say them a third time. With sincerity, with love, if that's possible. Trust the process: Let yourself hear these words, let them sink deep, to the wound's beginning. Let what happens, happen.

Imagine your father saying these words to you. See him in your mind's eye—his distinctive face with the tiny scar over his right eye, his Old Spice smell. Then look into his eyes as he looks into yours. And have him say the words. What are feeling? Can you just feel it? Can you feel the healing?

If your father is still alive, tell him what you have always wanted to hear from him. Ask him if he would be willing to say those words right now, right here…And then ask him the words he wanted to hear from *his* father, and maybe, his son.

New Warriors

I believe all men are born with Warrior energy. It is part of our make-up, who we are as men, and we can tap into our Warrior for the power and decisiveness we need to fulfill our mission in this world. We've been doing just that for thousands of years—using our Warrior energy to protect our women and children, our families, our community.

But our development as Warriors hasn't kept up with the times. The world is now so obviously interconnected, so internetted, so much bigger than just our families and our community…and yet much of our Warrior energy is still chauvinistically focused and shallowly expressed. Old Warriors are still running the show, yet the future belongs to New Warriors.

I grew up with a bunch of Old Warriors. My dad was an Old Warrior, and we watched movies together of Old Warriors—John Wayne, Charles Bronson, Clint Eastwood, George "General Patton" Scott. And we admired Old Warrior athletes like Jim Brown, Johnny Unitis, and Ben Hogan.

Old Warriors were men's men. Tough, driven, distant. Their Enemy was easily identifiable: those men in the other color uniforms, the Bad Guy in black, the Indians, the Communists. Their goals were simplistically clear: win championships; protect family and country; defeat Evil. And with a lock-and-load energetic intensity, with stoic perseverance, and with a truly impressive command of technology—guns, bombs, golf clubs—they single-handedly did just that. Often motivated by a righteous sense of revenge, these Old Warriors emitted a deep pain they never openly acknowledged. Somebody, somewhere had hurt them badly, I sensed, but they bit the bullet and never talked about that. Their bodies were powerful but expendable, and looking back was a waste of time—Forward, always forward, was their battle cry, and the faster the better.

And they're still around, these Old Warriors. There are the obvious oldies like Dick Cheney and Bobby Knight; there are "Weekend Warriors" galore. And hail to the fashionably re-packaged new Old Warriors like Michael Jordan, Lance Armstrong, Bret Farve, Arnold Schwarzenegger, and Mel Gibson.

I was deeply attracted to Old Warriors, but I never wanted to be an Old Warrior. In fact, somewhere, somehow, pretty early in my life, I unconsciously decided I would be exactly the opposite of an Old Warrior. OK, they often accomplished their goals—but Old Warriors did a lot of harm, Old Warriors were yellers and bullies, Old Warriors abused their power. Something was screwed up about those Old Warriors, so screw them, and the horse or the tank they rode in on!

I stuffed all my Warrior energy into a bag and buried it deep in my body. I threw the Warrior baby out with the bath water. I was a "soft male"—sensitive to the pain of others, often to the point of being a rescuer of those who I judged had been abused by Old Warriors.

That arrangement worked quite well for the first four decades of my life. Except for extremely rare outbursts, I was a model non-Warrior male: a Shadow Warrior. I was nice and caring, and people generally liked me. I was brilliant at anticipating the needs of others—friends, family, students, utter strangers—and satisfying them. Afraid of abusing power like I judged Old Warriors did, I relinquished much of my own power. I did an excellent job of taking care of everybody…but myself.

Through my New Warrior Training Adventure weekend, through my subsequent men's group, and through books like Gillette and Moore's *King Warrior Magician Lover*, I have gradually recovered my long-buried Warrior energy. I learned there was an option to being an Old Warrior: I could choose to be a New Warrior.

A New Warrior willingly adopts the virtues of the Old Warrior: A New Warrior is decisive and focused; he understands the necessity of discipline.

But rather than the Old Warrior's "power over," the New Warrior strives for "power with." And rejecting the increasingly sophisticated "killing" technology of the Old Warrior/Soldier, a New Warrior's metaphoric weapon of choice is the sword: precise, close, clean.

A New Warrior has a mission that extends beyond the Old Warrior's family/country/Good vs. Evil fundamentalism. A New Warrior's mission recognizes his connection to the rest of humanity, to the rest of the world, and to the earth. A New Warrior serves humanity, and not just a corporation or a country or a tyrant king.

A New Warrior understands he needs to first take care of himself in order to best take care of others. A New Warrior sets clear, clean boundaries. A New Warrior recognizes that his body is not only powerful but also wise.

A New Warrior knows his feelings, honors his feelings, and shares his feelings readily with others, including with men. A New Warrior transcends the Old Warrior's aloneness by embracing his connection to other men.

And a New Warrior isn't afraid to face the shadows of the past: he understands and experiences that releasing judgments and inviting forgiveness is the path of healing. He understands that the Enemy is not so much "out there" as within, and even that Enemy is not an enemy, but a part of himself that he can talk to and even bless.

New Warriors, I honor your Warrior energy. I honor your courage to face your own inner darkness, and to speak your feelings—from shame to joy. I honor your precision and your clarity; your ruthlessness in cutting to the heart of the matter. And I honor your compassion, even for the Old Warriors. You are strong, loving men. You will help create a strong, loving world. You are the Mandelas, the Ghandhis, and the Kings. You are New Warriors, you are the future, and I am proud of you.

The Blessing

♦

(For Tom Fitzpatrick)

Somewhere this side of manhood,
I missed a moment,
a tiny, small moment,
but one that would have assuaged
much of the son ache,
the aloof pain, the forty years
of father-hunger carved in my heart.

Here's what it would have looked like
    had it happened:

My father holding me in his Indian-brown arms,
looking me in the eye, father eyes to son eyes,
and moving his lips to words
he had never heard from his father
but had, miraculously, found somewhere—
under a magic rock or in a river,
maybe on the lips of a dream father
or from a group of warrior brothers,
holding me in his Indian-brown arms
    and saying:

Son, you have all you need
    to be a strong, loving man.
Son, you have all you need
    to be a strong, loving man.
Son, you have all you need
    to be a strong, loving man.

Not three times, really, this Father-to-Son,
but once with the profundity of three,
of three trillion, as every cell in my body
blooms with your words
and I feel the first solid stirrings of manhood—
    not just in my crotch
but in the catch of my heart,
in the tips of my fingers over skin,
in the tips of my toes over earth,
until my arms, my thin pale arms,
are Indian-brown like yours and strong enough
to hold my own son and say these words:

Son, you have all you need
    to be a strong, loving man.
Son, you have all you need
    to be a strong, loving man.
Son, you have all you need
    to be a strong, loving Man.

Circle complete,
    all of us complete,
        Blessings begun.

The New Founding Fathers

I come from a long line of Unblessed sons: my father, my father's father, *his* father...all the way back to the Mayflower.

And I suspect that's true for most men in America. A vicious cycle, like poverty or racism or alcoholism, of Unblessed son all but inevitably begetting Unblessed son. A nation of Unblessed sons led by Unblessed sons.

Until one day, one son breaks the cycle.

And on that day, beginning with that son, something miraculous happens: Blessed son begets...Blessed son. A new cycle, fed by strength and love rather than by shame and fear.

That part of the miracle I'm sure of. But I also speculate the healing happens backwards: that if I can find the way to Bless myself and to Bless my son, my father, inevitably, will be Blessed as well...and then his father, and his father's father...all the way back to the Mayflower.

And call me crazy, but I think the miracle is even bigger than that: when a magic number of sons are Blessed by these pioneer fathers, these new Founding Fathers, then this whole nation becomes the powerful, loving nation it was born to be.

And it doesn't stop there, this miraculous Blessing. The new Founding Fathers of this nation reach out to the new Founding Fathers of other nations...until we live in a world truly founded on strength and love—a world of Blessed Sons where all of us are connected, and all of us are Blessed.

Epilogue

Blessing Henry
(born June 8, 2005)

The first thing I did,
you still gooey on your mama's belly,
umbilical cord uncut,
the hospital world whirling around
our sudden oasis of white space,
was to take your tiny hands in mine
and give you The Blessing:

*Henry Michael James, you have all you need
to be a strong, loving man.*

And then, right there,
in your mane of black hair
    like my father's hair, like mine;
in your Indian skin, proud nose, and perfect lips;
in your feisty limbs and full voice
you passed the strong love back
in an Old School give-and-go
until suddenly I felt like the Blessed one:
in you, Henry, I see my history and my future;
in you, Henry, I am Blessed father and Blessed son.

APPENDIX

Writing Your Way Toward The Blessing

Our fathers are buried in the deep linings of our mind and the deep tissues of our body. And what stays buried cannot be Blessed. Writing can help resurrect parts of our father—the good, the bad, the beautiful, the ugly. To write about our fathers is to remember our fathers, to understand them—and ultimately, to forgive and to love them, as we simultaneously remember, understand, forgive, and love ourselves. Through this process, writing moves to Blessing.

So I encourage you to put down any fear you have—about exploring your father and his relationship with you, about writing—and pick up a pen. To help you get started, I will offer three different writing experiences: (1) Two random prompts—*"Dad, I remember_____/10 Questions About My Father*; (2) Three letters—*"Dear Dad"/"Dear Son"/"Dear Future Son*; and (3) A series of questions directly connected to the fourteen chapters of the book.

Of course, you could write on all of them, one of them, none of them. And you can do them at anytime. Whatever you do, I have a strong suggestion to ignore spelling, grammar, and all of that red pen nonsense that will keep you frozen up in your head. Instead, just write. I call this Freewriting, and Freewriting only has one rule: **Don't Stop Writing!** Set a timer for five minutes…and write non-stop until you hear ding!ding!ding! Or write non-stop until you get to the bottom of the page. If you get stuck—and you will, everyone does, no problem—write "Stuck, Stuck, Stuck"…until you get unstuck. The essential thing is to keep going, keep your pen moving. I have been teaching writing for twenty years, and Freewriting is the best way I know of to tease out deep, meaningful moments—to move from the static in our heads to the juice in our hearts.

Will this writing be painful? Probably. And joyous too. Working a deep sliver toward the surface is a painful process—but in the long-run, it's a healing operation. The writing you do here will move you toward forgiveness, toward love, toward The Blessing.

If you are currently in therapy, this could be excellent fodder for your next session. Or it might be healing self-therapy. If, however, the stuff that comes up is exceptionally weighty for you, please stop and find someone you can share it with, preferably a trained therapist.

Finally, I would be honored to read any of the writing that comes out of this for you. Please email me at: ppblessing@earthlink.net.

Ok. Time to dive in.

I. "Dad, I Remember_____" & 10 Questions

"Dad, I remember____": This prompt is a fast, relatively painless way to bring up father memories—to begin the remembering that blossoms into Blessing. Just repeat it at the beginning of every line—and see what comes up for you. Write as many as you can in five minutes, or write out 10 quick ones. And by the way, you don't have to start with "Dad"; it could be Daddy, Pops, Old Man, Frank, Asshole—whatever works for you.

Here's a sample:

Dad, I remember when you tossed our toys out the dormer window on Cortland Dr.
Dad, I remember the strength of your back.
Dad, I remember summer evenings on the Mohawk golf course.
Dad, I remember the talk about inviting Donna S. to the Junior Prom.
Dad, I remember your cheeks fat with mom's oatmeal cookies, and then, later, with steroids.
Dad, I remember the smell of leather and partridge blood on your hunting clothes.
Dad, I remember the way you crossed your legs and didn't care if you looked like a girl.
Dad, I remember your hands.

"10 Questions: Answering the ten questions below is another rapid way to air out long-buried father memories, as well as to stimulate imaginative healing possibilities. Make your responses as short, or as long, as you'd like. Feel free to skip any questions that don't grab you. Again, to get out of your head and into your heart, I suggest you write quickly, Freewriting whatever first comes to you.

(Note: I ask my questions in the past tense. I realize many of our fathers are still alive. I am referring to childhood, the early years, when the father-son pattern was forged.)

1. *What smells do you associate with your father?*
2. *When you picture your father, what one or two details stand out for you? What was his favorite piece of clothing?*
3. *What was your father's favorite thing to eat? To drink?*
4. *What was your father's favorite word or phrase or saying or joke?*
5. *If your father were an animal, what animal would he be?*
6. *What specific songs or music did your father listen to, dance to, whistle, or sing while you were growing up?*
7. *What I remember about my father's penis is _____?*
8. *If you had to choose one item or object that symbolized your father, what would you pick?*
9. *If asked to put a hand on the part of your body where your father wounded you, where would you place it?*
10. *If asked to put a hand on the part of your body where your father blessed you, or you wish your father would bless you, where would you place it?*

II. Letters

A letter to your father and a letter from your father—as well as a letter to your own son or future son—is a wonderfully personal way to speak the blessed words that, for most Unblessed sons, have never been spoken.

A) *A letter to your father*: Start out "Dear Dad" (or Daddy, Pops, Dickhead, Joe, etc.) and let the letter take you where it takes you. Maybe to all the things you wanted to say to your father that you've never had the chance to say. The angry things. The loving things. The gratitude and the disgust. The broken promises, terrific advice, cowardly disappearances, surprising returns…Tell him what you need him to know, get it out, all of it, the good, the bad, the beautiful.

B) *A letter from your father to you*: "Dear Son…" Step into your father's shoes for fifteen minutes or so, and let him write to you, his son, from his heart. Let him tell you all the good, the bad, and the truthful of his fatherhood; all the mixed-up love and shame.

C) *A letter from you to your son, or your future son*: As a father, or a future father, or a man with Father energy, write a letter to your son—or to some specific Unblessed son in your life. Tell him anything you want: tell him what you love about him, hope for him—give him The Blessing. Tell him about your successes, failures, and fears of being a father. Paint for him your best memory of the two of you together, past or future—that camping trip to Lake George, the moment at the zoo when the giraffes appeared, the time when he was less than a year when you held him over your head like a trophy and danced in the streets because the Pistons were World Champs! As always, write fast, and trust your heart will give you the words.

III. Chapter Prompts

These prompts, as noted, will follow the structure of the book. It may help to go back and read a particular section and see what comes up for you—what arises about your life, your father as you read: "Reading the story about the lamp reminds me of the time my step-dad threw this wrench at me while we were working on his Buick..." And you're off and writing with no need for further prompting. If you need a more directed stimulus, the following questions lend themselves to some heart-felt Freewriting.

> I. When in your life did you feel like an Unblessed son? Is there one incident in particular that stands out for you? Take five minutes and paint that moment: Freewrite all the details you can remember from it.
>
> II. How do you fill up your "Hole"—what is your addiction or addictions? Do you see any tie to this addiction and not getting The Blessing? What were your father's addictions?
>
> III. Given the basic emotions of Mad, Sad, Glad, Fear, Shame, which one of these do you feel the most comfortable expressing? The least? Which one did your father express the most and least?
>
> IV. What part of your body do you feel best about? What part of your body is the most shameful for you? What did you learn from your father—what he said, what he did—about men's bodies, about your body?
>
> V. Are you a Good Boy, a Bad Boy, an Eternal Boy, a Mama's Boy? Do you see how your role evolved from the dad-mom dynamics of your childhood?

How has this role played itself out in your life—and is it working for you now?

VI. When did you become a man? What was the "initiation" like? Did your father have a role in it?

VII. Do you have Unblessed brothers, or Unblessed uncles, or Unblessed cousins? Are you sympathetic, or not, to their Unblessedness? Is there someone in your family, perhaps a grandfather or an uncle or older brother or even a friend of the family, who Blessed you while growing up? Can you remember a specific incident where you received their Blessing?

VIII. Who were your heroes growing up? What, specifically, did you admire about them? What did they teach you about what it is to be a man?

IX. What have you been carrying around all these years in your Shadow Bag? What is hidden, denied, repressed? And what is your hidden Gold—Gold that you might be projecting on to the heroes of the last question, Gold that you have not yet owned?

X. Do you believe that finding the Right Woman will make you whole, will "complete" you? Have you looked to women to give you The Blessing? Have you cursed women because they didn't give you The Blessing, or because they cursed or shamed you? How did your mother bless you?

XI. Where have you felt connected to men? Have you ever been part of a Circle of Men—a space where men can come together and talk authentically about their lives? If you haven't been, how do you think being part of such a Circle would impact your life?

XII. What blessings, however small, did your father or some father figure give you? Can you recall several specific incidents where you felt blessed by men?

XIII. Regardless of whether or not you are presently a father, where does fatherhood rank in what you want to do in your life? What, for you, are the essentials of being a good father, and what fathers do you know (yourself included) who are living out these essentials with their children?

XIV. Is there an Unblessed son in your life—your own son, a lost kid in the neighborhood, a man at work, your father—who you have the love and the power to Bless? If so, what will you say to him, what can you do—and when will you do it?

Select Bibliography

Barton, Edward Read. *Mythopoetic Perspectives Of Men's Healing Work: An Anthology for Therapists and Others.* Bergin & Garvey, 2000.

Bly, Robert. *A Little Book on the Human Shadow.* Edited by William Booth. HarperSanFrancisco, 1988.

_____. *Iron John: A Book About Men.* Vintage Books, 1990.

Clothier, Peter. *While I Am Not Afraid: Secrets Of A Man's Heart.* In Word Press, 1998.

Corneau, Guy. *Absent Fathers, Lost Sons: The Search for Masculine Identity.* Shambhala, 1991.

Duvall, Jeffrey. *Stories of Men, Meaning, and Prayer: The Reconciliation of Heart And Soul In Modern Manhood.* Four Directions Press, 2001.

Eldredge, John. *Wild at Heart: Discovering The Secret of A Man's Soul.* Thomas Nelson, 2001.

Hollis, James. *Under Saturn's Shadow: The Wounding And Healing Of Men.* Inner City Books, 1994.

Levoy, Gregg. *Callings: Finding and Following an Authentic Life.* Three Rivers Press, 1997.

Meade, Michael. *Men and the Water of Life: Initiation and the Tempering of Men.* HarperSanFrancisco, 1993.

Moore, Robert and Douglas Gillette. *King Warrior Magician Lover: Rediscovering the Archetypes of the Mature Masculine Personality.* William Morrow, 1991.

Osherson, Samuel. *Finding Our Fathers: The Unfinished Business Of Manhood.* Free Press, 1986.

Pittman, Frank, M.D. *Man Enough: Fathers, Sons, and the Search for Masculinity.* Perigee, 1993.

Real, Terrence. *I Don't Want To Talk About It: Overcoming The Secret Legacy of Male Depression.* Scribner, 1997.

978-0-595-37733-6
0-595-37733-5